Exploring English GRAMMAR

Credits

Illustrations: Laurie Conley, Michael Fink, Marty Husted, Margaret Lindmark, Eva Vagreti, Chris Vallo

ISBN 978-1-5240-0269-5

Copyright © 2017 The Continental Press, Inc.

No part of this publication may be reproduced in any form or by any means, electronic, mechanical, photocopying, recording, or otherwise, without the prior written permission of the publisher. All rights reserved. Printed in the United States of America.

Table of Contents

Introduction to *Exploring English Grammar* 5

UNIT 1 Sentences
- Lesson 1 Sentences, Fragments, and Run-On Sentences 6
- Lesson 2 Subjects and Predicates 8
- Lesson 3 Types of Sentences 10
- Lesson 4 Conjunctions and Interjections 12
- Lesson 5 Compound Subjects and Predicates 14
- Lesson 6 Compound Sentences 16
- Lesson 7 Direct and Indirect Objects 18

UNIT 2 Nouns
- Lesson 1 Nouns: Proper, Concrete, and Abstract 20
- Lesson 2 Plural Forms of Nouns 22
- Lesson 3 Collective Nouns 24
- Lesson 4 Possessive Nouns 26

UNIT 3 Verbs
- Lesson 1 Action Verbs 28
- Lesson 2 Linking Verbs and Predicate Nouns and Adjectives ... 30
- Lesson 3 Helping Verbs 32
- Lesson 4 Subject-Verb Agreement 34
- Lesson 5 Simple Tense 36
- Lesson 6 Progressive Tense 38
- Lesson 7 Perfect Tense 40

UNIT 4 Pronouns
- Lesson 1 Pronouns 42
- Lesson 2 Pronouns: Possessive, Indefinite, and Interrogative ... 44
- Lesson 3 Pronouns and Antecedents 46
- Lesson 4 Reflexive and Intensive Pronouns 48

UNIT 5 Adjectives and Adverbs
- Lesson 1 Adjectives and Articles 50
- Lesson 2 Comparing with Adjectives 52
- Lesson 3 Adverbs and Intensifiers 54
- Lesson 4 Comparing with Adverbs 56

UNIT 6 — Phrases, Clauses, and Complex Sentences

Lesson 1	Prepositional Phrases	58
Lesson 2	Appositives	60
Lesson 3	Complex Sentences	62
Lesson 4	Compound-Complex Sentences	64
Lesson 5	Adjective Clauses	66
Lesson 6	Adverb Clauses	68
Lesson 7	Noun Clauses	70
Lesson 8	Misplaced and Dangling Modifiers	72

UNIT 7 — Capital Letters

| Lesson 1 | Sentences and Quotations | 74 |
| Lesson 2 | Proper Nouns, Proper Adjectives, and Titles | 76 |

UNIT 8 — Punctuation and Style

Lesson 1	End Punctuation and Other Uses of a Period	78
Lesson 2	Commas	80
Lesson 3	Apostrophes	82
Lesson 4	Quotation Marks	84
Lesson 5	Direct and Indirect Quotations	86
Lesson 6	Colons and Semicolons	88
Lesson 7	Hyphens, Dashes, and Parentheses	90

UNIT 9 — Choosing the Right Word

Lesson 1	Homophones	92
Lesson 2	Avoiding Double Negatives	94
Lesson 3	Misused Words	96
Lesson 4	More Misused Words	98
Lesson 5	Knowing the Difference	100

UNIT 10 — Writing Letters

Lesson 1	Writing a Thank-You Note	102
Lesson 2	Writing an Invitation	104
Lesson 3	Writing a Business Letter	106
Lesson 4	Addressing an Envelope	108
Lesson 5	Writing an Email	110
Lesson 6	Writing a Review	112

Grammar Handbook 114

Introduction to Exploring English Grammar

You use language every day to speak, listen, read, and write. Using language effectively helps you to communicate your thoughts and ideas to those around you. To understand and use the English language, you must understand and use the rules of grammar. Knowing parts of speech, punctuation, sentence structure, and capitalization rules helps you to master the English language. *Exploring English Grammar* reviews important language rules to help you grow into a skillful communicator.

Exploring English Grammar includes skills in the following areas:

- Sentence structure
- Nouns
- Verbs
- Verb tenses
- Pronouns
- Adjectives
- Adverbs
- Types of sentences
- Capitalization
- Punctuation
- Word usage
- Letter writing

UNIT 1: Sentences
Sentences, Fragments, and Run-On Sentences

Remember A **sentence** tells a complete thought. A **fragment** does not tell a complete thought. If two or more thoughts run together with no punctuation to separate them, the group of words is a **run-on sentence**.

Sentence The Hill of Tara was the seat of the high kings of Ireland.

Fragment Was the seat.

Run-On Located in County Meath, the Hill of Tara was used for ancient rituals it plays an important role in Irish mythology.

Corrected Run-On Located in County Meath, the Hill of Tara was used for ancient rituals. It plays an important role in Irish mythology.
OR
Located in County Meath, the Hill of Tara was used for ancient rituals; it plays an important role in Irish mythology.

Think About What are two ways to correct a run-on sentence?

_____

_____

Read and Apply Read the groups of words. Write **S** above the first word of each sentence. Write **F** above the first word of each fragment. Underline each run-on.

St. Patrick is the patron saint of Ireland. At 16 years old. Taken captive in Ireland. After he escaped, he returned home to England later, he went back to Ireland as a missionary. Many legends and myths. It is said that Patrick drove all the snakes out of Ireland. Defied the High King. The Irish people began to accept Patrick he is now considered a representation of the country. St. Patrick's Day is celebrated on March 17, the supposed day of his death throughout Ireland, it is both a sacred holiday and a cultural celebration.

© The Continental Press, Inc. **DUPLICATING THIS MATERIAL IS ILLEGAL.**

Write About

Write a paragraph about a cultural celebration in which you have taken part. It may be a St. Patrick's Day celebration or another holiday. Use complete sentences.

_____
_____
_____
_____
_____
_____
_____
_____
_____
_____

Review

Read each fragment or run-on sentence. Rewrite the groups of words as complete sentences. You may need to add words and punctuation marks.

1. Located in Europe.

   _____

2. The Republic of Ireland was once part of Britain the country declared its independence as the Irish Free State in 1921.

   _____
   _____

3. This popular tourist destination.

   _____

4. Many people think of leprechauns, shamrocks, and green the country also is full of stone castles, rolling hills, and quaint villages.

   _____
   _____

© The Continental Press, Inc. **DUPLICATING THIS MATERIAL IS ILLEGAL.**

Subjects and Predicates

Remember A sentence has two main parts: the **subject** and the **predicate.** The **complete subject** tells who or what the sentence is about. The **simple subject** is the noun or pronoun in the complete subject.

Many <u>people</u> enjoy listening to opera music.

The **complete predicate** tells about the subject. The **simple predicate** is the verb or verb phrase in the complete predicate.

The <u>audience</u> <u>listens</u> to the music in amazement.
<u>They</u> <u>are</u> excited to hear the next song.

Sometimes the subject follows the predicate or interrupts it.

On the stage stood a <u>woman</u>. There were <u>dancers</u> behind her.

Think About How can you identify the subject when it is not the first part of a sentence?

_____

_____

Read and Apply Read the sentences. Underline the simple subject in each sentence. Circle the simple predicate in each sentence.

  Opera tells a story through music and singing. Elaborate scenery fills the stage. Talented actors wear intricate costumes. However, the beautiful music commands the attention of the audience. Opera singers with years of training and experience fill the hall with their voices. There are no microphones used to amplify the sound. Instead, the singers learn to project their voices. In front of the stage sits the orchestra. From the instruments flow the musical notes. Have you seen an opera performance? You might be surprised by the music. Many famous opera pieces are used in commercials and television shows.

Write About Write a paragraph about a stage performance you have seen. Underline the complete subject in each sentence. Circle the complete predicate in each sentence.

_____
_____
_____
_____
_____
_____
_____
_____

Review Read each sentence. Underline the complete subject. Circle the simple subject.

1. Over the memorial hangs an American flag.

2. The dog on the leash barked loudly.

3. There were pieces of dirt lying on the floor.

Read each sentence. Underline the complete predicate. Circle the simple predicate.

4. After the storm, we opened the windows.

5. The mug with the crack leaked coffee on the floor.

6. On top of the desk sat a pile of papers.

Lesson 3: Types of Sentences

Remember A **declarative sentence** states something. It ends with a **period (.)**. An **interrogative sentence** asks something. It ends with a **question mark (?)**. An **imperative sentence** gives a command or makes a request. It can end with a period or an **exclamation point (!)**. An **exclamatory sentence** shows strong feeling. It ends with an exclamation point.

Declarative Vincent van Gogh painted many landscapes and still lifes.
Interrogative Where was van Gogh born?
Imperative Look at this beautiful painting.
Exclamatory How colorful it is!

Think About Which type of sentence is most commonly used? Why do you think so?

_____

_____

Read and Apply Read the sentences. Above each one, write **decl.** if it is declarative, **inter.** if it is interrogative, **imp.** if it is imperative, or **excl.** if it is exclamatory.

Who was Vincent van Gogh? During his lifetime, he was a poor painter who received little recognition. How that has changed! Today, he is considered one of the greatest painters in history. Look at this painting called *The Starry Night*. Van Gogh himself considered it a failure. How could that be? It is now one of the most well-known paintings in the world.

Van Gogh was part of the Post-Impressionist movement. What was that movement? What varied styles it covers! Artists explored different ways of showing their emotions through their paintings. Look at the bold colors and brush strokes in van Gogh's work. Observe the soft colors in other paintings.

© The Continental Press, Inc. **DUPLICATING THIS MATERIAL IS ILLEGAL.**

Write About

Write a paragraph about a painter or painting that you admire. Use at least one of each type of sentence.

_____
_____
_____
_____
_____
_____
_____
_____
_____

Review

Listen to each sentence. Circle **DECL** if it is a declarative sentence, **INTER** if it is an interrogative sentence, **IMP** if it is an imperative sentence, and **EXCL** if it is an exclamatory sentence.

1. DECL   INTER   IMP   EXCL
2. DECL   INTER   IMP   EXCL
3. DECL   INTER   IMP   EXCL
4. DECL   INTER   IMP   EXCL
5. DECL   INTER   IMP   EXCL
6. DECL   INTER   IMP   EXCL
7. DECL   INTER   IMP   EXCL
8. DECL   INTER   IMP   EXCL

Conjunctions and Interjections

Remember A **conjunction** joins words or groups of words. A **coordinating conjunction** joins ideas of equal importance.

Coordinating Conjunctions
We wanted to go on a picnic, <u>but</u> it rained all day.
We ate our sandwiches <u>and</u> apples in the kitchen.

A **subordinate conjunction** connects an independent and a dependent clause. Some subordinate conjunctions are *after, even if, before,* and *unless.*

Subordinate Conjunctions
<u>If</u> we get there early, we will find the best seats.
We must wait <u>until</u> Maria is ready.

An **interjection** is a word or group of words that shows strong feeling.

Interjections <u>Ouch!</u> A bee stung me!   <u>Yum</u>, this tastes good.

Think About When should you use an exclamation point after an interjection?

Read and Apply Read the sentences. Underline each conjunction. Write **C** over the coordinating conjunctions. Write **S** over the subordinate conjunctions.

Many adults and children recycle and reuse because they want to take care of the earth. Paper, glass, aluminum, and metal can all be recycled, but some people just throw these things away. If they are recycled, they are used to make new items. This helps save Earth's resources, so they will not run out. Composting, or breaking down natural waste, is another way to recycle. Many food scraps, grass clippings, and leaves can be composted. Place these things in an area of your yard or garden. Over time, they decompose and make a rich fertilizer. When your compost is ready, mix it back into your flowerbeds or garden.

© The Continental Press, Inc.   **DUPLICATING THIS MATERIAL IS ILLEGAL.**

Write About   Write a sentence using each of the interjections in the box. Use coordinating and subordinate conjunctions in your sentences, too.

| oh | aha | whoops | shh | hey |

1. _____
   _____

2. _____
   _____

3. _____
   _____

4. _____
   _____

5. _____
   _____

Review   Underline the conjunction or interjection in each sentence. Write **C** over the coordinating conjunctions. Write **S** over the subordinate conjunctions.

1. Yikes! There is a lot of trash on this beach.

2. The plastic bags and aluminum cans get in the ocean.

3. Sea animals get caught in them or try to eat them.

4. They die because they become sick from the trash.

5. Wow, that is terrible!

6. Whenever I am here, I always clean up my trash.

© The Continental Press, Inc.   **DUPLICATING THIS MATERIAL IS ILLEGAL.**

Lesson 5: Compound Subjects and Predicates

Remember A **compound subject** has two or more simple subjects. A **compound predicate** has two or more simple predicates. They use conjunctions.

Compound Subject A jacket, a woolen hat, and a red scarf were on the bench.

Compound Predicate Someone took them off and left them there by mistake.

Think About Look at the examples again. What are the simple subjects in the first sentence? What are the simple predicates in the second sentence?

_____

_____

Read and Apply Read the sentences. Underline the compound subject or compound predicate in each one.

Muscle strengthening and aerobic activity are important forms of exercise. People who want to build muscles use free weights and apply body weight. They curl ten-pound dumbbells in their hands or do push-ups on the floor. Pull-up bars and kettlebells are great tools for muscle strengthening. Exercises with these pieces of equipment increase muscle strength and build muscle mass.

People who do aerobic activities run, walk, and ride bike. These forms of exercise raise the heart rate and pump oxygenated blood to the muscles. Dancing, hiking, and swimming keep a person's breathing rate up for more than a few minutes. Cardio activities make your heart stronger and help control your weight. A fit body and a healthy mind require both forms of exercise.

© The Continental Press, Inc. **DUPLICATING THIS MATERIAL IS ILLEGAL.**

Write About Write a paragraph about what types of aerobic, or cardio, activities you enjoy.

_____
_____
_____
_____
_____
_____
_____
_____
_____
_____

Review Complete each sentence by writing a compound subject or a compound predicate.

1. The flowers in the garden _____.

2. _____ performed on the stage.

3. All of the students _____.

4. _____ rode the roller coaster.

5. The building on Main Street _____.

6. _____ grow in the garden.

Compound Sentences

Remember A simple sentence has one subject and one predicate. A **compound sentence** is two related simple sentences joined by a coordinating conjunction.

Simple Sentences
The sky was dark.
Raindrops were starting to fall.

Compound Sentence
The sky was dark, and raindrops were starting to fall.

Think About How do compound sentences help you make your writing more interesting?

_____

_____

Read and Apply Read the sentences. Underline each compound sentence.

The lightning strikes, and then, after a few moments, the thunder crashes. The closer the lightning is to you, the sooner you will hear the thunder. Sound is a vibration, and it travels through matter by making a chain of vibrations. Sound must make the air next to your ear vibrate, or you will not hear it. Sound travels in waves from the source. It moves through solids, liquids, and gases. Sound waves travel through air at about five seconds per mile, but they travel faster through water and steel.

Light travels faster than sound, but there are not many other things that do. When a machine, usually an airplane, travels faster than the speed of sound, it breaks the sound barrier. Normal airplanes do not travel this fast, but supersonic jets do. When a supersonic jet breaks the sound barrier, it makes a sonic boom. This loud noise sounds like thunder, and it can break windows!

© The Continental Press, Inc. **DUPLICATING THIS MATERIAL IS ILLEGAL.**

Write About Write a paragraph about an experience you had where you moved at a high speed. Use at least three compound sentences.

_____

_____

_____

_____

_____

_____

_____

_____

_____

_____

_____

Review Read each pair of simple sentences. Use a conjunction to combine them into a compound sentence.

1. I wanted to wear my new shirt. It was in the dirty laundry.

   _____

   _____

2. The lights began to flash. The singer came on stage.

   _____

   _____

3. Take the cookies out of the oven. They will burn.

   _____

   _____

4. We hiked up the mountain on the Creekside Trail. We came down using a different one.

   _____

   _____

Direct and Indirect Objects

Remember A **direct object** is the noun or pronoun that receives the action of an action verb. It answers the question *what?* or *whom?* An **indirect object** receives the direct object. It sometimes appears in a prepositional phrase. It answers the question *to whom?*, *for whom?*, or *for what?*

indirect object ↓   ↓ direct object
Jasper built his cousin a playhouse.

Jasper built a playhouse for his cousin.
direct object ↑   ↑ indirect object

Think About Explain how asking yourself certain questions can help you identify the direct object and the indirect object.

_____
_____
_____

Read and Apply Read the sentences. Underline the direct objects and indirect objects. Write **DO** above the direct objects. Write **IO** above the indirect objects.

Writer Marjory Stoneman Douglas described the Everglades as a "river of grass." This national park is an enormous swamp in southern Florida. Sea turtles, manatees, and Florida panthers, three endangered animals, make their homes in the Everglades. Park rangers monitor the animals' activities. Sea turtles build nests and lay eggs on the beaches. Panthers hunt prey and feed their young the meat. Many tourists visit the Everglades to see the manatees. These large marine animals eat sea plants and swim through the shallow waters. This unique ecosystem needs protection. Conservation groups preserve it for future generations.

Write About Write a paragraph about an endangered animal. Underline and label the direct objects and indirect objects that you write.

_____
_____
_____
_____
_____
_____
_____
_____
_____
_____

Review Read each sentence. Write **DO** on the line if the underlined word is a direct object. Write **IO** if it is an indirect object.

1. Mr. Vaughn bought his daughter a gift.　_____

2. After school, we rode the bus home.　_____

3. Mom carried the bucket of water outside.　_____

4. Caleb lent money to Mia for a soda.　_____

5. Dad handed the credit card to the clerk.　_____

6. Before going to bed, I brushed my teeth.　_____

7. Ashlee painted Dave a picture.　_____

8. The squirrel buried the acorns in the yard.　_____

UNIT 2: Nouns

Nouns: Proper, Concrete, and Abstract

Remember A **noun** names a person, place, animal, or thing. A **proper noun** names a specific person, place, animal, or thing. **Concrete nouns** are those that you can see or touch. **Abstract nouns** are ones you cannot see or touch. They are often ideas or feelings.

Proper Nouns	General Grant	Yellowstone National Park	Rover
Concrete Nouns	man	playground	hamburger	elephant
Abstract Nouns	pain	friendship	bravery	kindness

Think About Explain the difference between a concrete noun and an abstract noun.

_____

_____

Read and Apply Read the sentences. Circle the concrete nouns that are not proper nouns. Underline the proper nouns. Underline the abstract nouns twice.

Yusra Mardini had dreams of competing in the Olympic Games. The swimmer lived and trained in Damascus, a city in Syria. Her country was full of conflict and violence. Yusra feared for her safety, so she and her sister left. They traveled through Lebanon and Turkey. From there, they planned to cross the Aegean Sea to Greece. The girls climbed in a boat with 18 other people. The tiny craft was too full, and, out in the sea, it began to sink. Only four passengers could swim. They jumped in the water and pulled the boat behind them. They finally reached land, but Yusra continued on to Berlin where she began training again. In 2016, she competed in the Summer Olympic Games in Brazil on a team of refugees. Yusra hopes that someday peace will return to her homeland and that the citizens will be able to live without fear.

© The Continental Press, Inc. **DUPLICATING THIS MATERIAL IS ILLEGAL.**

Write About

Write a paragraph about a dream that you have for your future. Use at least one abstract noun and two proper nouns. Label these nouns.

_____
_____
_____
_____
_____
_____
_____
_____

Review

Listen to each noun. Circle **CONCRETE** if it is a concrete noun. Circle **PROPER** if it is a proper noun. Circle **ABSTRACT** if it is an abstract noun.

1. CONCRETE   PROPER   ABSTRACT
2. CONCRETE   PROPER   ABSTRACT
3. CONCRETE   PROPER   ABSTRACT
4. CONCRETE   PROPER   ABSTRACT
5. CONCRETE   PROPER   ABSTRACT
6. CONCRETE   PROPER   ABSTRACT
7. CONCRETE   PROPER   ABSTRACT
8. CONCRETE   PROPER   ABSTRACT

Lesson 2: Plural Forms of Nouns

Remember A **singular noun** names one. A **plural noun** names more than one. To make most nouns plural, add *s* or *es*. For some nouns, you must change a letter before adding *s* or *es*. Some plural forms are irregular.

Singular	uncle	bench	party	loaf	tooth	moose
Plural	uncles	benches	parties	loaves	teeth	moose

Uncountable nouns cannot be counted with numbers. They are treated as singular nouns and do not have a plural form.

Uncountable	rain	garbage	honey	money

Think About How can you decide if a noun is an uncountable noun or not?

_____

_____

Read and Apply Read the sentences. Find the four incorrect plural forms. Put a line through each one and write the correct form above it. Underline the uncountable nouns.

In the late 1800s, two newspaper companyes were at war with each other. Joseph Pulitzer's *New York World* and William Randolph Hearst's *New York Journal* both wanted to be the best. Out of this fight came an increase in yellow journalism. This term refers to false or greatly exaggerated news. Reporters focused on crime stories, thiefs, and conspiracies. The press quoted expertes who knew very little about subjects. Journalists faked interviews. Men and women were drawn in by sensational headlines. Sales climbed as more people bought newspaperes. The two rivals spent much of their lives trying to outdo each other.

Write About Write sentences using the plural forms of the words in the box. Use at least one word in each sentence. You do not need to use all the words.

| cactus | mouse | wolf | series | scarf | trout |
| daisy | lunch | box | river | visitor | sheep |

1. _____
   _____
2. _____
   _____
3. _____
   _____
4. _____
   _____
5. _____
   _____
6. _____
   _____

Review Write the plural form of each word. If the noun is uncountable, write **NO** on the line. Use a dictionary if you need help.

1. foot _____
2. half _____
3. fungus _____
4. foreman _____
5. dirt _____

6. church _____
7. rice _____
8. bus _____
9. spy _____
10. swine _____

Lesson 3: Collective Nouns

Remember A **collective noun** names a group of people or things.

Collective Nouns   team   troop   class   herd

Most of the time a collective noun refers to the group acting as a whole. Then it is a singular noun. Use a singular verb and a singular pronoun, when needed. When a sentence refers to the individuals in the group acting on their own, the noun is plural. Use a plural verb and a plural pronoun. Be consistent; do not change from singular to plural in the middle of a sentence.

Singular The <u>team</u> <u>wins</u> <u>its</u> game!
Plural The <u>team</u> <u>change</u> out of <u>their</u> uniforms and <u>go</u> home.
Incorrect The team change out of its uniforms.
The team changes out of their uniforms.

Think About How can you decide if a collective noun is singular or plural?

_____

_____

Read and Apply Read the sentences. Underline the collective nouns.

John Barry went to sea as a young boy, and, at age 21, he received command of his first ship. When the American Revolution began, he was given the job of outfitting the Continental Navy. The British fleet was the strongest in the world. The Continental Congress trusted Barry to put it to the test. Barry fought bravely throughout the war. On March 8, 1778, he led an attack against the British. Barry's squadron consisted only of small boats, but it captured three British ships. Barry had a reputation for caring about his crew. He always made sure the men had proper provisions. After the war, Barry captained a merchant ship. In 1797, President George Washington and the Senate asked Barry to serve his country again by building a permanent navy.

© The Continental Press, Inc. **DUPLICATING THIS MATERIAL IS ILLEGAL.**

Write About Have you ever spent time on a boat or a ship? Write a paragraph about your experience. If you have not, write a paragraph imagining what it would be like to live on a ship.

_____
_____
_____
_____
_____
_____
_____
_____
_____

Review Read the sentences. Write **S** if the collective noun is singular. Write **P** if it is plural.

1. The committee is meeting on Tuesday.   _____

2. Throughout the year, the faculty each give a presentation.   _____

3. My sister's dance troupe rehearses at the studio.   _____

4. This band will play its new song at the concert.   _____

5. Our class is going on a field trip.   _____

6. The family are arriving at different times.   _____

Possessive Nouns

Remember A **possessive noun** names who or what has something. It shows ownership or connection. Add an apostrophe and an *s* to make a singular noun or a plural noun that does not end in *s* possessive. Add an apostrophe only to a plural noun that ends in *s*.

Karen's notebook   the bears' food   the sheep's pen

Think About How do you use an apostrophe to show possession?

_____

_____

Read and Apply Read the sentences. Underline each singular possessive noun. Circle each plural possessive noun.

In the United States, the president's wife is called the First Lady. A first lady's job is important. These women are much more than their husbands' advisors and supporters. When the nation was young, the wife's main role was as the White House's hostess. Through the years, many first ladies have begun to champion their own causes. Michelle Obama's goal was to end childhood obesity. Laura Bush's efforts focused on education. Nancy Reagan's campaign was against drugs. Other first ladies' projects included the environment, historical preservation, and women's suffrage.

Before moving to America's capital, some first ladies had other jobs. Betty Ford worked as a dancer, and Ida McKinley was a manager in her father's bank. After Eleanor Roosevelt's time in the White House, she became the United Nations's first delegate.

Some presidents' nieces, sisters, or daughters have filled this vital role. In the future, we may see our country's first "First Gentleman."

Write About Write a paragraph about a cause that is important to you. How would you promote your cause?

_____
_____
_____
_____
_____
_____
_____
_____
_____
_____

Review Complete each sentence by writing the correct possessive form of the word below the line.

1. This afternoon, the _____ mayor will give a speech.
   city

2. The _____ petals are beginning to drop.
   flowers

3. This _____ antlers measured 80 inches across.
   moose

4. After its victory, the _____ ranking rose to first place.
   team

5. Next week, the gallery will display several _____ paintings.
   artists

6. When geese molt, the _____ feathers are replaced with new ones.
   geese

Lesson 1

UNIT 3: Verbs
Action Verbs

Remember An **action verb** tells what a noun does or did.

  decide   crashes   asked   tried   broke

If an action verb has a direct object, it is **transitive.** If it does not have a direct object it is **intransitive.**

Transitive   Cameron <u>paints</u> a picture.
Intransitive   He <u>paints</u> well.

Think About What is a direct object?

Read and Apply Read the sentences. Underline the action verb or verbs in each one. Then write **T** above each transitive verb. Draw an arrow to the noun that receives its action. Write **I** above each intransitive verb.

According to legends, King Arthur ruled England in the 5th century. First, Arthur's father, King Uther Pendragon, governed the nation. After King Uther died, many men claimed the right to be the next king. The wizard Merlin sealed a sword in a stone. The person who pulled the sword from the stone would reign as king. All the men tried, but they failed. Then Arthur easily slid the sword from the stone. Merlin crowned Arthur as the king.

During his reign, Arthur gathered brave knights around him. These gallant men fought courageously, performed chivalrous deeds, and completed difficult quests. Arthur built his castle at Camelot. From there, he and his queen, Guinevere, led the country.

Write About Write a paragraph about a time you did something brave.

_____
_____
_____
_____
_____
_____
_____
_____
_____

Review Read each sentence. Underline the action verb or verbs and label each one with **T** for transitive or **I** for intransitive.

1. The students wore costumes and recited their lines.

2. I watch my dog run through the backyard.

3. A hawk swooped through the air and landed in the tree.

4. After school, Rachel completed her homework.

5. My little cousin crawled carefully across the floor.

6. Kurt races around the track and crosses the finish line.

Lesson 2: Linking Verbs and Predicate Nouns and Adjectives

Remember A **linking verb** connects the subject of a sentence to words in the predicate. It shows what the noun is or how it appears.

| is | was | seems | tasted | look | sounded |
| are | were | appear | smell | felt | became |

A **predicate noun** follows a linking verb and refers back to the simple subject. A **predicate adjective** describes the simple subject.

Predicate Noun Dorothea Lange was a <u>photographer</u>.

Predicate Adjective Her pictures of poor families are <u>powerful</u>.

Think About Look at the sentences above. What are the linking verbs in the sentences? What is the simple subject in each sentence?

_____

_____

Read and Apply Read the sentences. Underline the linking verb in each one. Write **N** over each predicate noun. Write **A** over each predicate adjective.

Most deserts are hot, dry places with very little rainfall. Without much moisture in it, desert air is thin. For this reason, distant objects often appear closer. Faraway noises sound loud. After a short time in the dry desert air, your skin feels tight. You become thirsty very quickly. Even warm water tastes good then!

Today, almost a third of the world's land area is desert. That seems like a big number! Not all deserts are hot. The continent of Antarctica is a cold desert. The regions around Earth's poles look barren. They are dry because they receive very little precipitation.

© The Continental Press, Inc. DUPLICATING THIS MATERIAL IS ILLEGAL.

Write About

Write a paragraph describing the climate in which you live. Circle each linking verb in your sentences. Label any predicate nouns or predicate adjectives you use.

_____
_____
_____
_____
_____
_____
_____
_____
_____
_____

Review

Read each sentence. Write **PN** on the line if the underlined word is a predicate noun. Write **PA** if it is a predicate adjective.

1. Amy is a very talented <u>dancer</u>.   _____

2. This building was a <u>restaurant</u> at one time.   _____

3. After several failed attempts, I became <u>angry</u>.   _____

4. The air felt <u>cold</u> when I stepped outside.   _____

5. The students were <u>ready</u> for the test.   _____

6. Lions are fierce <u>hunters</u>.   _____

7. The village was just a tiny <u>dot</u> on the map.   _____

8. This chicken casserole tastes <u>salty</u>.   _____

Lesson 3: Helping Verbs

Remember   A **helping verb** comes before the **main verb** in a sentence. It helps the main verb express the action or show the connection. Together, the verbs form a **verb phrase**.

<u>will</u> clap	<u>have</u> sung	<u>was</u> sitting	<u>could</u> dance
<u>will be</u> done	<u>had been</u> reading	<u>were</u> driving	<u>may have</u> gone

Think About   Look at the helping verbs. Are these verbs always helping verbs? Can they be another type of verb?

_____

_____

Read and Apply   Read the sentences. Underline the verb phrases with helping verbs.

Parkour and freerunning are two similar activities, but skilled participants can tell the difference. Parkour was developed from military obstacle courses. A person who does parkour is called a traceur. A traceur will look at an area and must decide the fastest route between two points. He or she may use different ways to get between the two points. People could run; they might jump; they may vault over things. Some traceurs have climbed walls!

Freerunning was created after parkour. Freerunners have added acrobatic moves and tricks to their movements. Freerunning is considered more personal. A freerunner can express his personality through his fluid movements. No one should try freerunning and parkour without proper training.

© The Continental Press, Inc.   **DUPLICATING THIS MATERIAL IS ILLEGAL.**

Write About Write a paragraph about an activity that you enjoy doing outside. Use helping verbs and underline the verb phrases you write.

_____
_____
_____
_____
_____
_____
_____
_____
_____

Review Complete each sentence by writing a helping verb in the blank.

1. The reporter _____ asked a difficult question.

2. During the track meet, Trevor _____ race in three events.

3. We _____ driving for six hours.

4. Dad _____ painting the living room.

5. The car _____ made a strange noise.

6. Bella _____ stayed after school.

7. Jameson and Kylie _____ hiking the mountaintop trail.

8. The Bears _____ winning the game.

Subject-Verb Agreement

Remember   The verb in the predicate must agree with the simple subject. Use a singular verb for a singular subject. Use a plural verb for a plural subject.

The birds sit on the fence. After a moment, a robin flies away.

When the subject is *one, every, each, neither, either, everyone, nobody, somebody,* or *everybody,* use a singular verb.

Everyone at the table wants a glass of water.

When a compound subject uses the conjunction *and,* use a plural verb. If it uses the conjunction *or,* use a singular verb, unless the subjects are plural.

Doug and Rushil row the boat.

A white shirt or a blue sweater matches those pants.

Flowers or vegetables grow well here.

Think About   How do you decide what verb form to use in a sentence?

_____

Read and Apply   Read the sentences. Circle the correct verb for each sentence.

Most organs in your body [has   have] only one function. Your heart [pump   pumps] blood. You [breathe   breathes] with your lungs. Your stomach and small intestine [break   breaks] down food.

Everyone [has   have] a liver, but not many people [know   knows] its important functions. The liver [perform   performs] four main activities. First, it [make   makes] bile. This chemical [goes   go] into the small intestine, where it [dissolves   dissolve] fat in food. The liver [stores   store] many food compounds. When body cells [needs   need] energy, the liver [supply   supplies] it from the stored food. As its third job, this organ [filters   filter] germs and poison from your blood. Finally, this amazing chemical factory [produces   produce] many important substances the body needs to work.

© The Continental Press, Inc.   **DUPLICATING THIS MATERIAL IS ILLEGAL.**

Write About

Write a paragraph about an important job that you have. Make sure that your subjects and verbs agree.

_____
_____
_____
_____
_____
_____
_____
_____

Review

Read each sentence. Underline the simple subject. Write **S** over it if it is singular; write **P** over it if it is plural. Then circle the correct verb form.

1. Anyone with a blue ticket [sit   sits] in this section.

2. Newspapers and magazines [print   prints] stories about celebrities.

3. The basketball players [dribble   dribbles] the balls.

4. Neither of these trees [grow   grows] quickly.

5. Mom or Dad [pack   packs] my lunch every morning.

6. One of the girls [kick   kicks] the ball into the goal.

7. Your hat and scarf [is   are] on the chair.

8. The musicians [practice   practices] every day.

Lesson 5: Simple Tense

Remember   A verb form indicates when the action takes place: the past, the present, or the future. Use the plain or *s*-form of a verb in **present tense**. Use the helping verb *will* before the verb in **future tense**. Add *ed* to most verbs in **past tense**. Some verbs are irregular, so they have different past-tense forms.

Present Tense   Ms. Stanford teaches the lesson. The students listen carefully.

Future Tense   Ms. Stanford will teach the lesson. The students will listen carefully.

Past Tense   Ms. Stanford taught the lesson. The students listened carefully.

Maintain the same tense within a sentence and paragraph, unless the timing of the action changes.

Incorrect   Ian <u>raised</u> his hand and <u>asks</u> to leave the room.

Think About   Look at the last example again. Write this sentence correctly.

_____

Read and Apply   Read the sentences. Find the five verbs that are incorrect. Cross out each verb and write the correct form above it.

In 1783, a Frenchman become the first human to ride in a hot air balloon. Two years later, two men flied a hot air balloon across the English Channel. In the first hot air balloons, riders burned items on board to make enough heat for the balloon to rise. During America's Civil War, both sides used hot air balloons. Soldiers in balloons creates maps of battlefields. They directed artillery fire and observed enemy troops.

Today, many people enjoy hot air balloon rides for fun. Colorful balloons filled the morning and evening skies and drift over the countryside. Balloon enthusiasts attend festivals. Will hot air balloons change in the future? Maybe people will thought of new uses for this aircraft!

© The Continental Press, Inc.   **DUPLICATING THIS MATERIAL IS ILLEGAL.**

Write About Write a paragraph describing a real or fictional ride in a hot air balloon. Write in past, present, or future tense. Maintain the tense throughout your paragraph.

_____
_____
_____
_____
_____
_____
_____
_____
_____

Review Complete each sentence by writing the correct form of the given verb. Write *past, present,* or *future* on the line to tell when the action takes place.

1. As I climbed the stairs, I _____ the painting. _____
   notice

2. Tomorrow, Roberta will _____ dinner for us. _____
   cook

3. The pool _____ for the season today. _____
   open

4. Mom _____ carefully in the snow until we got home. _____
   drive

5. Tim _____ his bike to the park, where I met him. _____
   ride

6. The band will _____ a new song. _____
   record

© The Continental Press, Inc. **DUPLICATING THIS MATERIAL IS ILLEGAL.**

Progressive Tense

Remember **Progressive tense** uses a form of the helping verb *be* and the **present participle** of the main verb. The present participle is the *ing*-form of the verb. Use the correct tense of *be* to show past, present, or future progressive tense.

Past Progressive	I was typing a text.	The boys were running.
Present Progressive	I am typing a text.	The boys are running.
Future Progressive	I will be typing a text.	The boys will be running.

Think About How do you know if the progressive tense verbs describe action in the past, the present, or the future?

_____

_____

Read and Apply Read the sentences. Find the five mistakes with helping verbs or present participles. Cross out each mistake and write the correct word above it.

In the 1920s, a group of people is talking about making a trail. They were proposing one that would run 2,650 miles from Canada to Mexico along the western coast of the United States. Through the 1930s, they were scouting a route and makeing plans. The Pacific Crest Trail (PCT) was being born.

Today, hundreds of thousands of people are hiking this trail every year. Some are spending only a day or two on the trail. Others are taking on the entire trail from end to end. Thru-hikers were carrying their supplies on their backs. They are sleeping under the stars. People are traveling the PCT for years to come. Groups are workking to preserve the trail for future generations.

Write About Write a paragraph about what you think it would be like to hike the Pacific Crest Trail.

_____
_____
_____
_____
_____
_____
_____
_____
_____

Review Read each sentence. Write the correct form of *be* and the present participle of the given verb on the line. Use context clues to decide if the sentence should be written in past, present, or future progressive tense.

1. The movie _____ at 4:00 and 7:15 tomorrow.
   show

2. We _____ to stop at the store later.
   plan

3. In November, my grandparents _____ to Florida.
   move

4. I _____ my bedroom when I found my missing earring.
   clean

5. While the judges talked, the gymnasts _____ for the scores.
   wait

6. As always, my sister _____ a lot of questions.
   ask

© The Continental Press, Inc. **DUPLICATING THIS MATERIAL IS ILLEGAL.**

Perfect Tense

Remember **Perfect tense** uses the helping verbs *have, has,* and *had* with the **past participle** of the main verb. For most verbs, the past participle is the same as the past tense.

Past Perfect Tense	had built	had asked
Present Perfect Tense	has stopped	have bought
Future Perfect Tense	will have remained	will have flowed

Some past participles of irregular verbs are different than the past tense.

Past Tense	came	went	gave	chose
Past Participle	come	gone	given	chosen

Think About How do you know if the past participle is different than the past tense form of the verb?

_____

_____

Read and Apply Read the sentences. There are four incorrect past participles. Cross out the incorrect word and write the correct word above it.

French settlers had first came to Canada in 1604. The French king had given them permission to start a colony there. At first, the colonists had gotten along well with the native people. Sometimes they had argued, but more often they had traded in friendship. By 1650, though, the French had fought several wars with the Iroquois. In the cold Canadian climate, many food crops had grew poorly. Some discouraged colonists had given up and had moven back to France. But others had put down roots and soon had built cities. By 1688, the French population of Canada had risen to about 10,000.

Write About

Write a sentence correctly using the given pronoun.

1. ours
   _____

2. whose
   _____

3. everything
   _____

4. several
   _____

5. which
   _____

6. her
   _____

Review

Listen to each sentence. Circle **POSSESSIVE** if the pronoun in the sentence is a possessive pronoun. Circle **INDEFINITE** if it is an indefinite pronoun. Circle **INTERROGATIVE** if it is an interrogative pronoun.

1. POSSESSIVE   INDEFINITE   INTERROGATIVE
2. POSSESSIVE   INDEFINITE   INTERROGATIVE
3. POSSESSIVE   INDEFINITE   INTERROGATIVE
4. POSSESSIVE   INDEFINITE   INTERROGATIVE
5. POSSESSIVE   INDEFINITE   INTERROGATIVE
6. POSSESSIVE   INDEFINITE   INTERROGATIVE

Pronouns and Antecedents

Remember The noun that a pronoun stands for is called its **antecedent.** It should be close to its pronoun to avoid confusion.

↓ antecedent for *him* and *he*
Roy Chapman Andrews was an explorer. Fossils fascinated him. In the 1920s, he visited the Gobi Desert.

Use a singular pronoun with a singular antecedent. Use a plural pronoun with a plural antecedent.

Incorrect Roya dropped their book.
Correct Roya dropped her book.

Think About How can you avoid confusing pronouns?

_____

_____

Read and Apply Read the sentences. Underline each pronoun. Then draw an arrow from the pronoun to its antecedent. Circle the two confusing pronouns.

Chief Joseph was the leader of the Nez Perce tribe. As settlers moved into Oregon territory, they took more and more land that had belonged to them. Chief Joseph wanted peace, but he also wanted his people's land. The American government told Joseph that he must move his people to a reservation. A group of warriors attacked some settlers, and Joseph and his people were forced to flee. The tribe attempted to get to Canada, but the army pursued it. Food ran out and it was cold. When Joseph saw that his people were dying, he finally surrendered. The Nez Perce people were moved to Oklahoma, where they were forced to make their home. Joseph never stopped pleading for the return of his homeland.

© The Continental Press, Inc. **DUPLICATING THIS MATERIAL IS ILLEGAL.**

Write About Rewrite each sentence to clarify the confusing pronoun usage. You may need to add or change words or change word order. There is more than one way to correct each sentence.

1. Nobody remembers their locker combinations.
   _____

2. While the students listened to the guest speakers, they took notes.
   _____
   _____

3. All of the boys left his baseball gloves at the field.
   _____

4. Since he knows a lot about cars, Ryan and Tanner changed its oil.
   _____
   _____

5. They said we cannot go outside for recess because it is storming.
   _____
   _____

6. Raoul told Jared that he was wrong.
   _____

Review Fill in the circle next to each sentence that shows correct pronoun and antecedent agreement.

○ After Becky and Rick finished dinner, they washed the dishes.
○ Each scout proudly wore her badges.
○ When Freddy visited his grandmother, he helped them clean the attic.
○ Every player on the team has their own equipment.
○ The family ate its picnic lunch, and then they went swimming.
○ The dog must wear its collar when it is outside.

Reflexive and Intensive Pronouns

Remember A **reflexive pronoun** refers back to the subject of the sentence. The antecedent of a reflexive pronoun is the subject. An **intensive pronoun** is used for emphasis. It can refer to any noun or pronoun in the sentence.

Reflexive Pronoun   Andre taught <u>himself</u> to read music.
Intensive Pronoun   Each student received a letter from the principal <u>herself</u>.
   The headmaster <u>himself</u> presented the awards.

Think About What is the difference between reflexive and intensive pronouns?

_____
_____

Read and Apply Read the sentences. Underline the reflexive pronouns. Circle the intensive pronouns.

   Have you ever found yourself in an emergency medical situation? Many people learn basic first aid techniques themselves. The Heimlich maneuver clears an object that is choking a person. The choker himself will typically indicate that he is choking. Quickly get behind him and wrap your arms around his waist. Make a fist and place it slightly above the person's navel. Hold the fist with your other hand and make a quick, upward push. Repeat as needed. If you yourself are choking, perform this maneuver on yourself.

   An ambulance itself may take several minutes to arrive. Learn hands-free CPR for yourself to restart a person's heart. Put your hands over the person's heart and push in a steady rhythm. Continue until emergency technicians themselves arrive.

   Anyone can educate himself by taking classes to learn these important skills. We should all learn them for ourselves because we never know when we might need them.

Write About Write a paragraph about a time you had to react quickly in a situation.

_____
_____
_____
_____
_____
_____
_____
_____
_____

Review Read each sentence. Draw a line from the *self*-pronoun to its antecedent. On the line, write **R** if it is a reflexive pronoun. Write **I** if it is an intensive pronoun.

1. My baby brother is too young to feed himself. _____

2. I fixed the flat tire on my car by myself. _____

3. Rosita asked to see the chef himself about the bad food. _____

4. Xun met the lead actress herself. _____

5. Dan and I made ourselves lunch and ate on the patio. _____

6. The coaches themselves run with us at practice every day. _____

UNIT 5: Adjectives and Adverbs
Adjectives and Articles

Remember An **adjective** describes or modifies a noun or pronoun. The words *the, a,* and *an* are **articles,** special adjectives that signal a noun will follow.

A single white cloud floated in the blue sky.

A **demonstrative adjective** points out a noun. The words *this, that, these,* and *those* are demonstrative adjectives.

This plate is cracked, but those plates are fine.

A **proper adjective** is an adjective formed from a proper noun.

The Russian ballet company performed at a New York theater.

Think About What is the relationship between an adjective and a noun or pronoun?

Read and Apply Read the sentences. Underline all the adjectives and articles. Write **D** above the demonstrative adjectives. Write **P** above the proper adjectives.

In 1942, Anne Frank, a young German Jewish girl, received a beautiful, red, checkered diary as a birthday gift. She used that book to record her private thoughts. At this time, the European Jewish population was persecuted. Anne's family, with help from loyal friends, hid in tiny secret rooms for two long years. Anne kept an account of her thoughts and daily activities. The German secret police discovered Anne and her family. They were sent to horrible labor camps. Anne died a few short months before British troops freed the prisoners. Later, Anne's father found that precious diary and published it. Those people who read it are touched by Anne's powerful words.

© The Continental Press, Inc. **DUPLICATING THIS MATERIAL IS ILLEGAL.**

Write About   Rewrite each sentence by adding adjectives to modify the underlined nouns. Select adjectives to make the sentences more interesting.

1. The conductor bowed to the audience.

   _____

   _____

2. The dogs chased the fox up a tree.

   _____

   _____

3. The truck carried crates of oranges.

   _____

   _____

4. The girls ate cupcakes at the restaurant.

   _____

   _____

Review   Read the sentences. Circle any articles in each sentence. Look at the underlined adjective. If it is a demonstrative adjective, write **D** on the line. Write **P** if it is a proper adjective. Write **A** if it is neither of these.

1. An angry dog would not let anyone pass. _____

2. Could you hand me those keys? _____

3. This book has a section about Japanese cuisine. _____

4. An Australian swimmer set the world record. _____

5. The stone house on the corner was sold at an auction. _____

6. We admired the Spanish architecture in Seville. _____

© The Continental Press, Inc.   **DUPLICATING THIS MATERIAL IS ILLEGAL.**

Comparing with Adjectives

Remember To make the **comparative** and **superlative** forms of most short adjectives, add suffixes. Add *more, most, less,* or *least* before longer adjectives. Some adjectives have special comparative and superlative forms.

Adjective	icy	nice	gray	hopeful	good	bad
Comparative	icier	nicer	grayer	more hopeful	better	worse
Superlative	iciest	nicest	grayest	most hopeful	best	worst

Think About How do you decide which form of an adjective to use?

_____

_____

Read and Apply Read the sentences. Find the five incorrect comparing forms. Cross out each mistake and write the correct form above it.

Edward Teach, known as Blackbeard, was the more notorious pirate ever to sail. Although others were better pirates and captured greater numbers of ships, Blackbeard had the fearsomest reputation. He was more intelligent than other pirate captains. He built his reputation until he was more feared than anyone else. His victims often surrendered without a fight. Blackbeard grew a more larger fleet than others. He took riskier actions in order to trick other ships and capture them. Blackbeard's legends remain some of the famouser pirate stories. Hundreds of years later, Blackbeard is known as the best—or worse—pirate ever.

Write About   Choose three of the adjectives in the box. Write a sentence using the comparative form and one using the superlative form for those adjectives.

good	little	common	important	pale	mighty
happy	low	foggy	bold	swift	brave

1. comparative: _____
   _____

   superlative: _____
   _____

2. comparative: _____
   _____

   superlative: _____
   _____

3. comparative: _____
   _____

   superlative: _____
   _____

Review   Read each sentence. Circle the correct comparing form. Write **C** on the line if it is comparative. Write **S** if it is superlative.

1. Many people consider Michael Jordan the [greater   greatest] basketball player of all time. _____

2. Which of these cars has [less   least] horsepower? _____

3. The grilled chicken sandwich was clearly the [more popular   most popular] choice in the cafeteria. _____

4. Vegetables straight from the garden are [more flavorful   most flavorful] than those bought in the store. _____

Adverbs and Intensifiers

Remember An **adverb** describes or modifies a verb, an adjective, or another adverb.

    Verb   My mom <u>always</u> reminds me to do my best.

Adjective   Jamie is <u>normally</u> shy.

   Adverb   I <u>very</u> quickly pushed the door closed.

Some adverbs act as **intensifiers**. These words give stronger meaning or add emphasis to the word they modify.

I was <u>extremely</u> happy with the result of the game.

Brian was not <u>at all</u> interested in the salesman's product.

Think About Look at the first set of examples. What word does each adverb modify?

_____

_____

Read and Apply Read the sentences. Underline each adverb. Then draw an arrow from the adverb to the word it modifies.

    The Great Smoky Mountains National Park is located squarely on the border between Tennessee and North Carolina. The park is very aptly named for a mist that slowly blows across its peaks. The Cherokee people had lived peacefully in these mountains for many years, but they were cruelly forced from their homes in the 1830s. Settlers lived fairly primitively off the land. The logging industry quickly and completely changed the people's lives. Logging so rapidly depleted the forests in the early 1900s that the government finally stepped in. The Great Smoky Mountains National Park ensures the incredibly beautiful landscape will remain for years to come.

© The Continental Press, Inc. **DUPLICATING THIS MATERIAL IS ILLEGAL.**

Write About Rewrite each sentence by adding adverbs to modify the underlined words. You may use more than one adverb to modify a word.

1. People <u>volunteered</u> to prepare <u>delicious</u> food for the party.

   _____

   _____

2. Two dogs <u>romped</u>.

   _____

3. Hawks <u>glide</u> over the <u>tall</u> trees.

   _____

4. Alan <u>runs</u> late, but today he was <u>early</u>.

   _____

   _____

5. We <u>watch</u> the sky and <u>observe</u> the stars.

   _____

   _____

Review Read the sentences. Underline the adverb in each sentence. Write *how*, *when*, or *where* on the line to tell what information the adverb gives.

1. The Miller family left for vacation today.   _____

2. A large crowd anxiously watched the tightrope walker.   _____

3. Mom asked my brother to carry the clean laundry upstairs.   _____

4. The concert will begin soon.   _____

5. Keira jumped backward to avoid the falling branch.   _____

6. Mr. Green appears to be a highly likely suspect.   _____

© The Continental Press, Inc.   **DUPLICATING THIS MATERIAL IS ILLEGAL.**

Comparing with Adverbs

Remember The **comparative** and **superlative** forms of adverbs are made in the same way as the comparative and superlative forms of adjectives.

Adverb	hard	slowly
Comparative	harder	more slowly
Superlative	hardest	most slowly

Some adverbs have special comparative and superlative forms.

Adverb	well	badly	much	little	far
Comparative	better	worse	more	less	farther
Superlative	best	worst	most	least	farthest

Think About How do you make the comparing forms of adverbs?

_____

_____

Read and Apply Read the sentences. Circle the correct form of the adverb in each pair.

Jackie Joyner-Kersee could run the [faster   fastest] of any girl in East St. Louis, Illinois. She could jump [higher   highest] than most of the boys, too. She was great at many sports, but she performed [more superbly   most superbly] of all in track. After competing in four Olympic Games, she has won medals [more often   most often] than any other female track athlete. She broke records [more spectacularly   most spectacularly] than anyone else. Her best event was the long jump, where she jumped [farther   farthest] than the other competitors. Joyner-Kersee still holds the world record for the heptathlon. Four times, she did [better   best] than she had before and broke her own record. She set the current record in 1986 and it has lasted [longer   longest] than many other track records.

Write About Write a paragraph about an excellent athlete, past or present. Describe what he or she does well using comparative and superlative adverbs.

_____
_____
_____
_____
_____
_____
_____
_____
_____

Review Read the sentences. Write the correct form of the adverb that is under each line.

1. All dogs behave the _____ for their owners.
   well

2. Olivia arrived _____ than we did.
   early

3. The pianist played _____ than any of the other musicians.
   beautifully

4. Ted completed this crossword puzzle _____ than the first one.
   easily

5. I like lima beans _____ of all.
   little

6. Connor hit the ball the _____ and won the contest.
   hard

UNIT 6: Phrases, Clauses, and Complex Sentences

Prepositional Phrases

Remember A **preposition** is a word that relates a noun or pronoun to another word in the sentence. It is always part of a **prepositional phrase.** The noun or pronoun is called the **object of the preposition.** There can be a compound object of the preposition.

Our friends will be coming <u>to town</u> <u>before noon</u>.

<u>During the summer and fall</u>, Pedro works <u>at the greenhouse</u>.

Beth and I split the pizza <u>between us</u>.

Think About Should you use a subject pronoun or an object pronoun in a prepositional phrase? Explain.

_____

_____

Read and Apply Read each sentence. Underline each prepositional phrase. Circle each object of the preposition.

Trash is a problem for many communities across the country. Some places make energy from garbage. Through various processes, tons of garbage are turned into fuel. An anaerobic digester is a machine that uses natural processes to turn waste into useable energy. The best materials to use in an anaerobic digester are food waste, fats, oils, grease, and livestock manure. During anaerobic digestion, microorganisms act without oxygen to break down the waste. Through the process, biogas is created. This fuel can generate electricity in homes and buildings. Through anaerobic digestion, fertilizers are also created. Farmers and gardeners use it on their fields and gardens. Towns, communities, and businesses can all find value from this technology.

© The Continental Press, Inc.   **DUPLICATING THIS MATERIAL IS ILLEGAL.**

Write About Write a sentence using each of the given prepositions. Circle the object or objects of the preposition in each sentence.

1. beside
   _____

2. before
   _____

3. under
   _____

4. near
   _____

5. onto
   _____

6. by
   _____

Review Complete each sentence by adding a prepositional phrase. Underline the preposition. Circle the object of the preposition.

1. There was no mail _____ today.

2. We ate _____ for the first time.

3. _____, Harry went to sleep.

4. Marilyn climbed _____.

5. _____, the girls waited for their friends.

6. The horse leaped _____.

Lesson 2: Appositives

Remember An **appositive** is a word or group of words that explains or identifies the noun or pronoun that comes before or after it. An appositive is set apart from the rest of the sentence with commas.

<u>An American artist</u>, Georgia O'Keeffe is known for her desert landscape paintings.

She received the Presidential Medal of Freedom, <u>the highest honor given to an American citizen.</u>

Think About How is an appositive used in a sentence?

_____

_____

Read and Apply Read the sentences. Underline the appositive in each one.

Charlie Chaplin, a legendary actor and comedian, was born into poverty in London, England. A singer and performer, his mother encouraged his dream of acting. Chaplin joined a troupe, a group of traveling actors, when he was a young teenager. Mack Sennett, a film producer, saw Chaplin and signed him to an acting contract.

In the early 1900s, silent films, movies without dialogue, were the only type made. Chaplin created an iconic character, "The Little Tramp," and became a star. A kindhearted, bumbling character, the Little Tramp carried a cane and wore a boiler hat.

Chaplin thought that "talkies," movies that included dialogue, lacked the artistic beauty of silent films. In the 1930s, Chaplin made two of his most famous films, *City Lights* and *Modern Times,* as his last silent films.

© The Continental Press, Inc. **DUPLICATING THIS MATERIAL IS ILLEGAL.**

Write About Write a paragraph about a movie that has had an impact on you in some way. Use at least three appositives in your paragraph.

___

Review Combine each pair of sentences by making one of the sentences into an appositive.

1. Dora is a seventh grader. She won the 100-meter race.

2. We borrowed Dad's truck to move furniture. It is a large, blue pickup.

3. Johannes Vermeer was a Dutch painter. He painted *Girl with a Pearl Earring*.

4. The cruise ship leaves from Miami. It is a city in Florida.

Complex Sentences

Remember A **complex sentence** is made up of one independent clause and at least one dependent clause. A **clause** is a group of words in a sentence that has a subject and a predicate. An **independent clause** gives a complete thought. A **dependent clause** does not give a complete thought.

independent clause ↓   ↓ dependent clause
Jamilla plans to go to the gym after she stops at the bank.
Mason, who plays on the school's baseball team, wore his jersey to school today.

Think About What is the difference between a compound sentence and a complex sentence?

_____

_____

Read and Apply Read the sentences. Underline the complex sentences.

Because Alice Hamilton cared, factories are safer today. While Alice worked on her medical degree, she became interested in public health. At that time, many factories did not have standards in place for the safety and health of the workers. After Alice became a doctor, she began to study workers' diseases. She realized that people who worked in certain industries were susceptible to various illnesses. Workers in lead factories were slowly killing themselves as they breathed. For years, Alice studied the health effects caused by working with various chemicals, and her discoveries led to changes in factories. Alice received many awards for her work, and many lives have been saved because of her research.

Write About Write a paragraph about something that you would like to change. How can you go about changing it? Use at least two complex sentences.

_____
_____
_____
_____
_____
_____
_____
_____
_____
_____

Review Combine each pair of sentences to make a complex sentence. You may add words and change the order of the sentences.

1. Miss McNally is a fine jewelry maker. She likes to work with silver.

   _____
   _____

2. Hannah told a joke. Jill laughed.

   _____
   _____

3. The girl watched the speaker's lips. The girl was deaf.

   _____
   _____

4. The tide went out. The boat drifted away.

   _____
   _____

© The Continental Press, Inc. **DUPLICATING THIS MATERIAL IS ILLEGAL.**

Compound-Complex Sentences

Remember A **compound-complex sentence** contains two or more independent clauses and at least one dependent clause. The independent clauses are often joined by a conjunction. The dependent clause may be in the middle of one of the independent clauses.

When Mr. Hartford dismissed the class, Kelly went to her locker, and Jim walked to the bus stop.

My grandparents, who live on a farm, grow a lot of vegetables, but they do not have any animals.

Think About How can you use what you know about complex sentences and compound sentences to write compound-complex sentences?

_____

_____

Read and Apply Read the sentences. Underline the compound-complex sentences.

At one time, scientists classified fungi as plants. Once they recognized the important differences between plants and fungi, they placed fungi in its own category. Fungi, which includes mushrooms, yeast, and mold, get their food from decomposing matter, or they act as parasites to get food from a host. These organisms do not have seeds. Once a fungus becomes ripe, it releases spores, and the wind spreads these tiny eggs to new areas.

Fungi have many uses. Some mushrooms and yeast are used in foods, and other fungi are ingredients in medications that help fight diseases. In nature, fungi help decompose matter so important elements can return to the ground and the air. There are around 100,000 species of fungi, and mycologists, who are scientists specializing in studying fungi, continue to find new species.

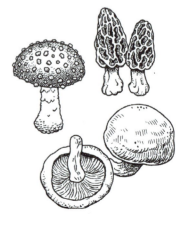

Write About Combine each group of sentences into a compound-complex sentence. There are multiple ways to combine the sentences. You may need to leave out repeated words, use pronouns, or make other changes.

1. For lunch, I ate a salad. It had delicious dressing on it. Then I took a walk.

   _____
   _____

2. The team arrived at the ballpark. They warmed up. They were ready when the game started.

   _____
   _____

3. Wash the dishes first. Clean your room. Then we can go out.

   _____
   _____

4. Leah hopes to travel to Italy someday. She reads everything she can find about the Italian culture. She is learning to speak Italian.

   _____
   _____

Review Read each compound-complex sentence. Underline the independent clauses once. Underline the dependent clauses twice.

1. Since rain fell all day, no one came to our yard sale, but we will have another one next week.

2. The neighbors repaired the playground after the storm caused a lot of damage, and now children can play there again.

3. Bonita's grandmother gave her a clock that had been in the family for almost a hundred years, so Bonita displayed it on her mantle.

Adjective Clauses

Remember A **clause** is a group of words that has a subject and a predicate. An **adjective clause** is a dependent clause that acts as an adjective in a sentence. It modifies, or describes, a noun or pronoun. It generally begins with a **relative pronoun**. An adjective clause is set off from the rest of the sentence by commas when it is not necessary for the sentence's meaning. Commas are not used when the clause is needed.

The soup <u>that Terry made</u> is delicious.

The soup, <u>which is on the stove</u>, is ready.

Think About How do you know when to use commas around an adjective clause and when not to use them?

_____

_____

Read and Apply Read the sentences. Underline the adjective clauses.

Mount St. Helens, which is located in Washington State, is an active volcano. The eruption that made it famous occurred on May 18, 1980. Geologists who had been studying the volcano knew that an eruption was coming. They had been charting activity and had issued warnings to the people who lived in the area. On the morning of May 18, an earthquake, which measured 5.1 on the Richter scale, started a massive landslide on the side of the mountain. A huge blast followed as the magma, which had been building up inside the mountain, was released. The damage that the eruption caused was extensive. Today, the scars still show, but plant life, which had been completely destroyed on the mountainside, has returned and is flourishing. Scientists whose jobs involve monitoring volcanic activity continue to watch Mount St. Helens.

Write About   Complete each sentence by writing an adjective clause. Use the relative pronouns in the box. Add commas if needed. Do not use any of the relative pronouns more than twice.

| who | whose | which | that | whom |

1. The dancer _____ is on the stage.

2. Mrs. Sasaki is the teacher _____.

3. *The Sound of Music* is a musical _____.

4. We visited Central Park _____.

5. My friend Hiroko _____ plays the saxophone.

6. The police officer _____ asked the witness some questions.

Review   Read the sentences. Look at the underlined adjective clauses. Circle the noun or pronoun that each one modifies.

1. The athlete whom I admire most is Lou Gehrig.

2. The book, which you ordered last week, has just arrived.

3. Anyone who parks here will get a ticket.

4. Neighbors helped the family whose home had been damaged by fire.

5. The window that is broken doesn't open.

© The Continental Press, Inc.   **DUPLICATING THIS MATERIAL IS ILLEGAL.**

Lesson 6: Adverb Clauses

Remember An **adverb clause** is a dependent clause that acts as an adverb in a sentence. It tells when, where, why, or how. An adverb clause can come before or after the independent clause and usually begins with a word such as *after, although, as, because, before, if, like, since, than, though, unless, until, when,* or *while*.

The town clock struck three <u>as we left school</u>.

<u>Since it was my birthday</u>, I baked a cake.

Think About Look at the examples again. How do the adverb clauses modify the verbs?

_____

_____

Read and Apply Read the sentences. Underline the adverb clauses.

Since scientists had never seen a platypus before, they thought it was a joke. This unusual animal looks like a mix of several other animals. Like a duck, it has a bill and webbed feet. Its tail is wide and flat like a beaver's tail. It has a smooth, furry body like an otter. The platypus swims easily underwater when it hunts for food. It scoops up insects, worms, and other food as it moves along the bottom of a river. Though the platypus is an excellent swimmer, it cannot stay completely underwater for very long.

Although it is a mammal, the platypus lays eggs. A female burrows deep into a tunnel when she is ready to lay her eggs. After the eggs hatch, she stays with the tiny babies until they are able to swim.

A male platypus squirts out toxic venom if it feels threatened. Platypuses move around more at night because they are nocturnal. These fascinating creatures live in Australia, where they survive in both warm and cool climates.

© The Continental Press, Inc. **DUPLICATING THIS MATERIAL IS ILLEGAL.**

Write About Write six sentences that contain at least one adverb clause. Use the words in the box to begin the adverb clauses. Do not use any word twice.

| after | if | when | as soon as | anywhere | even if | where |
| like | as | unless | until | while | because | since |

1. _____

2. _____

3. _____

4. _____

5. _____

6. _____

Review Read the sentences. Look at the underlined adverb clauses. Circle the word it modifies.

1. Since it was Halloween, Greg read a scary story.

2. The barn roof fell because no one repaired it.

3. As soon as the alarm rang, the firefighters leapt into action.

4. We cannot leave until Rita is ready.

5. My brother is taller than I am.

Noun Clauses

Remember A **noun clause** is a dependent clause that acts as a noun in a sentence. It can be either the subject or an object in the sentence. Noun clauses often begin with one of these words.

what	how	who	whom	when
that	whoever	whomever	why	where

How anyone can climb mountains is a mystery to me.

Show Linda what you made.

I will speak to whomever answers the phone.

Think About What is the role of the noun clause in each of the examples?

_____

_____

Read and Apply Read the sentences. Underline the noun clauses.

Why some whales sing interests many scientists. They know that whales use complex sounds to attract mates. Whales use simpler noises to tell each other where food is located or which way they should travel. Whatever noises a whale makes carry through the water almost four times faster than in the air.

Whoever hears a humpback's song can hear the beauty of the music. This "singer" creates an intricate composition of moans, cries, and howls. Scientists have learned that all the whales in an area typically sing different versions of the same song. Where the whales live has an effect on the song. Whales in the Atlantic Ocean sing a different song than those in the Pacific or Indian Oceans. We may never know how humpback whales compose their songs or what they are saying to each other.

Write About

Write two sentences that contain a noun clause as a subject. Write two that contain a noun clause as an object.

Noun clause as a subject

1. _____

2. _____

Noun clause as an object

3. _____

4. _____

Review

Read the sentences. Underline the noun clause in each one. Write **S** on the line if the noun clause is the subject. Write **O** if it is an object.

1. Whom Mala bought the present for is a mystery. _____

2. That Calvin stayed awake through the whole movie was amazing. _____

3. Let me show you what I bought at the farmer's market. _____

4. Whoever answers the question correctly is the winner. _____

5. The reporter explained why the accident happened. _____

6. I do not know where this path leads. _____

Misplaced and Dangling Modifiers

Remember A **modifier** is a word or group of words that tells more about a thing or action. It should be placed as close as possible to the word it modifies. **Misplaced modifiers** cause confusion because they are too far away from the word they modify.

Misplaced Modifier   Under his bed, Aaron found his book.
Corrected   Aaron found his book under his bed.

Dangling modifiers do not clearly belong with any word in the sentence.

Dangling Modifier   Looking at the exhibits, his hat got lost.
Corrected   Looking at the exhibits, he lost his hat.

Think About How is a dangling modifier different from a misplaced modifier?

_____

_____

Read and Apply Read the sentences. Underline the six misplaced or dangling modifiers. Write **M** over the misplaced modifiers. Write **D** over the dangling modifiers.

Mary Mallon became known as "Typhoid Mary" after doctors discovered that she had infected many people with typhoid inadvertently. Working as a cook, the virus transferred from Mary to the people who ate her food. Although Mary was healthy and had never had the disease, she was a carrier of the disease. Easily spread through food or water, many people became sick.

No one explained to Mary why she should be evaluated. Taken by force, they arrested her. Doctors performed tests and found the virus in Mary's body quickly. Unable to understand why she was targeted, the authorities made Mary live in isolation for the rest of her life.

© The Continental Press, Inc.   **DUPLICATING THIS MATERIAL IS ILLEGAL.**

Write About
Rewrite each sentence from Read and Apply that contains a misplaced or dangling modifier. Correct the misplaced or dangling modifiers.

_____
_____
_____
_____
_____
_____
_____
_____
_____
_____

Review
Fill in the circle next to each sentence with a dangling or misplaced modifier.

○ At the party, Enzo wore a mask only.

○ Cleaning out my room, my missing library book was discovered.

○ When the clowns entered, Chula excitedly clapped her hands.

○ After arriving at the mall, a parking spot was found.

○ Biking along the road, Jen saw a deer.

○ I put the drinks in the refrigerator for the party.

UNIT 7: Capital Letters
Sentences and Quotations

Remember The first word of a sentence begins with a capital letter. The pronoun *I* is always written as a capital letter, too.

Last year, I competed in our school's spelling bee.

Begin the first word of a **direct quotation** with a capital letter.

"Will you compete this year?" Mason asked. "Maybe you will win!"

"Yes, I think I will," I answered, "but I need to study."

Think About In a direct quotation, how do you know which words should begin with a capital letter when part of the quotation comes after the conversation word?

_____

_____

Read and Apply Read the sentences. Circle the letters that should be capitalized.

the Metropolitan Museum of Art is the largest art museum in the United States. opened in 1870, the Met, as it is often called, includes art spanning thousands of years.

"my favorite section of the Met," Lisa said, "is the Egyptian art."

"what type of Egyptian art do they have there?" asked Hudson.

lisa responded, "there are tapestries and ornate pieces of jewelry. the Egyptians made beautiful stone jars, and the carvings on them often tell a story. my sister and i also enjoy looking at the mummies!"

one of the most famous pieces in the Met's Egyptian collection is a small blue-green statue of a hippopotamus. nicknamed "William," this figure is made from a ceramic material and decorated with images of river plants. it was found in an Egyptian tomb and is over 4,000 years old.

© The Continental Press, Inc. **DUPLICATING THIS MATERIAL IS ILLEGAL.**

Write About

Write a paragraph about a museum that you have visited. Include a direct quotation from yourself about it. Use capital letters correctly.

_____
_____
_____
_____
_____
_____
_____
_____
_____

Review

Fill in the circle next to each sentence that shows correct capitalization.

- ○ This year, Mr. Gorman directed the school play.
- ○ the library has Story time every Wednesday morning.
- ○ "Let's ride the bumper cars," said Juan, "and then let's do the waterslide."
- ○ "We need gas in the car," said Mom, "Before we can go to Grandma's."
- ○ once i finish my homework, i will do my laundry.
- ○ My friend Sarah plays piano, and I like to sing.
- ○ Emily asked, "will there be a band at the dance?"
- ○ "This park has great hiking trails," said Liam. "We come here often."

© The Continental Press, Inc.   **DUPLICATING THIS MATERIAL IS ILLEGAL.**

Proper Nouns, Proper Adjectives, and Titles

Remember Proper nouns and proper adjectives begin with capital letters. If the proper noun is made up of two or more words, each main word begins with a capital letter. People's names sometimes include a **title,** which is written with a capital letter.

Proper Nouns

Ms. Ella Monroe   President Woodrow Wilson   Georgia

Park Street   October   Labor Day   The Sweet Cafe

Proper Adjectives   the Canadian border   a British ship

The first word, last word, and each main word of the **title** of a work begin with a capital letter. Underline or italicize the titles of longer works. Put the titles of shorter works in quotation marks.

The Fellowship of the Ring   "The Star Spangled Banner"

Think About When are words like *president, street,* or *the* capitalized and when are they not?

_____

_____

Read and Apply Read the sentences. Circle each word that should be capitalized. Underline or put quotation marks around each title.

anne, emily, and charlotte brontë were three british authors and poets. The sisters lived quiet lives in yorkshire, england, in the early 1800s. At the time, women were rarely able to publish their own writings, so the sisters used male names: acton, ellis, and currer bell.

anne wrote two novels and numerous poems. Her most famous novel, the tenant of wildfell hall, is now considered one of the classics of english literature. emily's only novel, wuthering heights, shocked many readers when it was published. Two of her poems, no coward soul is mine and remembrance, are now considered great pieces. The oldest sister, charlotte, achieved the most fame. Her novel jane eyre is read and taught around the world.

Write About Write a paragraph about one of your favorite authors. Give the titles of some of the author's books, poems, or stories.

_____
_____
_____
_____
_____
_____
_____
_____
_____

Review Write each group of words using correct capitalization. Underline or put quotation marks around titles.

1. saturday, april 29

2. the barber of seville, an italian opera

3. shakespeare's romeo and juliet

4. the japanese city of tokyo

5. senator ellen parker

6. molly malone, an irish song

7. rodeo drive in beverly hills

8. the chrysler building

UNIT 8: Punctuation and Style
End Punctuation and Other Uses of a Period

Remember   A **period (.)** ends a declarative or imperative sentence. A **question mark (?)** ends an interrogative sentence. An **exclamation mark (!)** ends an exclamatory sentence or an imperative sentence that shows strong feelings.

We are at a baseball game. Look at the score.

Which player is up to bat?

How far that ball went! Hit a home run!

A period is used after an **initial** and after many **abbreviations**.

John Fitzgerald Kennedy = J. F. K.   January = Jan.

Think About   Not all abbreviations use a period. What are some abbreviations that do not end in a period?

Read and Apply   Read the sentences. Insert the correct end punctuation and additional periods where needed.

Have you ever taken a ride on the Mississippi The Mississippi R is the second longest river in North America It flows from L Itasca in Minnesota to the Gulf of Mexico How long is it Good question Different groups claim varying lengths for the river, but it is between 2,320 to 2,550 miles long

How important the Mississippi is It has been a vital means of transportation for hundreds of years Canoes, steamboats, barges, and cruise ships have traveled its waters

Read some stories about the Mississippi How many there are Samuel L Clemens, also known as Mark Twain, placed some of his most famous stories on the river The Mississippi River is a special part of America

© The Continental Press, Inc.   **DUPLICATING THIS MATERIAL IS ILLEGAL.**

Write About

Rewrite each group of words using an initial or an abbreviation for each underlined word. Use a dictionary if you need help.

1. Doctor Cassandra Anderson _____

2. Smart Company, Incorporated _____

3. North Chester Parkway _____

4. Mount Rainier, Washington _____

5. Wednesday, August 16 _____

6. General Colton Reyes _____

7. 179 Madison Avenue, Northeast _____

8. 2 feet by 13 inches _____

9. Maryland Department of Education _____

10. Golden Gate Bridge in California _____

11. Eric Frederick Winston _____

12. Monday through Thursday _____

Review

Fill in the circle next to each sentence that shows the correct use of end punctuation, initials, and abbreviations.

○ Send this to Ms. Ann D. O'Malley in FL.

○ Have you been to St. Marys Rv. or Lak. Superior!

○ In Oct., we will visit Las Vegas, NV?

○ When will Maj. Hendrick give her speech?

○ How high Mt. Everest is!

○ Turn SE on Fifth Av. and then drive 3 mi.

Lesson 2: Commas

Remember A **comma (,)** has many uses. It separates the two independent clauses in a compound sentence. It comes before the conjunction.

Gabe wanted to hike the mountain, but the trail was unsafe.

It separates an appositive from the rest of the sentence.

Lake Baikal, the deepest lake in the world, is located in Asia.

It separates **coordinate adjectives,** which are adjectives that modify the same noun.

It was a long, hot, dark night.

Think About How can you summarize a comma's job?

Read and Apply Read the sentences. Put commas where they belong.

During the Great Depression a time of economic hardship in America Hoovervilles became common sights. Shanty towns built by the homeless these settlements were full of hungry unemployed people. Herbert Hoover was president when the Great Depression began so his name was attached to the towns. Residents built homes out of whatever materials they could find and many lived in cardboard or tin dwellings. These unstable weak haphazard shelters often needed to be rebuilt but their occupants had nowhere else to go. Franklin D. Roosevelt the governor of New York won the presidential election in 1932 and he quickly went to work improving the country's economy. Through the New Deal Roosevelt's recovery program people slowly returned to work and the grim dirty Hoovervilles began to disappear.

© The Continental Press, Inc. **DUPLICATING THIS MATERIAL IS ILLEGAL.**

Write About Write a paragraph about what you think it would have been like to live in a Hooverville. Use commas in each of the three ways shown in this lesson.

_____
_____
_____
_____
_____
_____
_____
_____
_____
_____

Review Fill in the circle next to each sentence that shows all the commas placed correctly.

○ The Mega Split, an ice cream sundae with three types of ice cream, is Sweet Treat's specialty.

○ A huge, long, black snake slithered through the grass.

○ The meteorologist, a young man, with glasses, predicted warm, sunny, weather next week.

○ Jane wanted to make oatmeal, but, she was out of milk.

○ Kaden might go to the Grand Canyon, or he will visit Philadelphia, a city, in Pennsylvania.

○ The scientist won the Nobel Prize in Chemistry, a prestigious, annual award.

Lesson 3: Apostrophes

Remember An **apostrophe (')** is used to take the place of the letter or letters that are left out of a **contraction.**

they are	cannot	he would	will not	she is
they're	can't	he'd	won't	she's

An apostrophe is used to make a noun possessive.

Michelle's book   the house's roof   the students' teacher

Think About The contraction *who's* means *who is*. It is often confused with the possessive pronoun *whose*. How can you remember the difference?

_____

_____

Read and Apply Read the sentences. Above each underlined word or group of words, write a contraction or a possessive phrase to replace it.

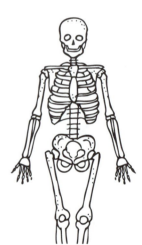

The body of a human baby has 270 bones. That number does not stay the same; by the time you are an adult, you have 206 bones. The skeletal system is a moving, growing part of a body of a human. The outer part of a bone has nerves and blood vessels that feed the bone. The next layer is the compact bone. It is hard and smooth. Next is a spongy layer called cancellous bone. The job of this layer is to protect the bone marrow. The many layers of cancellous bone are not as hard as the compact bone layer. They are lighter, too, which makes bones a little bendable. A bone is not brittle and will not break as easily. The center of a bone contains bone marrow. The purpose of the bone marrow is to produce red and white blood cells, which help to keep you healthy.

Write About Write a paragraph about another body system or part and how it helps you to stay healthy.

_____
_____
_____
_____
_____
_____
_____
_____
_____

Review Listen to each group of words. Write the correct contraction or possessive form.

1. _____

2. _____

3. _____

4. _____

5. _____

6. _____

7. _____

8. _____

Quotation Marks

Remember Quotation marks (" ") surround the exact words that a person says.

Lily said, "I need to stop at the library."

They are also used around the title of a short work, such as a story, poem, song, article, or TV show.

We sang "Old MacDonald Had a Farm" with the children.

Use **single quotation marks (' ')** inside double quotation marks.

Adam asked, "Have you read 'The Ransom of Red Chief' by O. Henry?"

"The principal said, 'School is closed on Friday,'" remarked Cong.

Think About In what situations do you use single quotation marks?

_____

_____

Read and Apply Read the sentences. Insert double or single quotation marks where needed.

Edgar Allan Poe is one of America's greatest authors. His stories and poems often reflect the losses he experienced in his own life.

Do you have a favorite Poe story? asked Cooper. I have read his poem The Raven. It is considered one of the greatest American poems. His poem Annabel Lee is very beautiful. It is sad, but it is more hopeful than many of his other works.

My favorite story is The Cask of Amontillado, replied Nora, but I also enjoyed The Tell-Tale Heart.

The Raven brought Poe fame during his lifetime, but his collected works have stood the test of time.

Write About

Interview a friend about his or her favorite story, poem, or song. Summarize your interview, including some direct quotations from your friend.

_____
_____
_____
_____
_____
_____
_____
_____
_____
_____
_____
_____
_____

Review

Fill in the circle next to each sentence that correctly uses quotation marks.

- ○ 'Our school chorus sang "The Little Birch Tree,' said Isabelle.
- ○ Evan recited "Mother to Son" during the performance.
- ○ "Dad said, 'The keys are on top of the refrigerator,'" replied Aleka.
- ○ "If I am ever on "American Idol,"" said Rico, "I will sing "Superstition.""
- ○ Jack London wrote 'The Klondyker's Dream' and 'To Build a Fire.'
- ○ "My sister likes to sing 'I Will Survive' very loudly," complained Kyle.

Direct and Indirect Quotations

Remember A direct quotation tells the exact words that a person said. Place quotation marks around the words. Place end punctuation and commas inside the quotation marks. Begin a new paragraph when the speaker changes.

John said, "We have practice after school."
"I will be there," said Gina, "after I ask Mrs. Thomas a question."
"I forgot my cleats!" exclaimed Drew.

An **indirect quotation** does not tell the exact words that a person said.

John said that we have practice after school.
Gina told me that she will be there after she talks to Mrs. Thomas.
I heard Drew say that he forgot his cleats.

Think About How are indirect quotations different from direct quotations?

Read and Apply Read the sentences. Underline the direct and indirect quotations. Write **D** above the direct quotations and write **I** above the indirect quotations.

"The Highland games celebrate the culture of Scotland," Eli said. "One of the most common games is the caber toss."

Kameyo asked what a caber is. So Eli told his friends that a caber is a long log. In the caber toss, the athlete picks up the caber and holds it vertically with the smaller end in his hand. He runs forward and tosses the caber so that it flips end over end. The larger end should hit the ground first.

"Wow! What other events are there?" said Kameyo.

Eli explained that the stone put is similar to the shot put event in track and field. The thrower launches a heavy ball from a standing position. The person who throws it farthest is the winner.

© The Continental Press, Inc. **DUPLICATING THIS MATERIAL IS ILLEGAL.**

Write About Write about a cultural event that you have attended. Include direct and indirection quotations from yourself or someone with whom you attended the event.

_____
_____
_____
_____
_____
_____
_____
_____
_____
_____

Review Read each sentence. Write **D** on the line if it is a direct quotation. Write **I** if it is an indirect quotation.

_____ "Have you ever seen a shooting star?" asked Chris.

_____ Jorge told Kelsey that he will be late on Tuesday.

_____ Brandon shouted, "I got it!"

_____ "After I finish my homework," Tamyra said, "I will ride my bike."

_____ Savonna wondered what time people were going to arrive.

_____ Reyna explained, "I can't dance because I hurt my foot."

Colons and Semicolons

Remember A **colon (:)** separates a list from the rest of a sentence. It is also used to separate the hour from the minutes in written time notation.

We saw interesting creatures at the aquarium: stingrays, jellyfish, clownfish, and sharks.

The aquarium opens at 9:00 AM and closes at 7:30 PM.

A **semicolon (;)** is used in place of the comma and conjunction in a compound sentence.

We looked at the displays before lunch; we watched the dolphin show after lunch.

Think About What is the difference between a semicolon and a colon when used in a sentence?

_____

_____

Read and Apply Read the sentences. Put colons and semicolons where they belong.

Clouds are divided into groups based on their height above the earth high clouds, middle clouds, low clouds, and clouds of vertical development. High clouds are wispy and thin they are located over 20,000 feet. There are three types of high clouds cirrus, cirrostratus, and cirrocumulus. Middle clouds are often gray they appear between 6,000 and 20,000 feet. Low clouds are located at 6,000 feet or lower they are called stratus clouds. These clouds are usually gray and often bring rain or snow. Clouds that extend vertically can reach different levels in the sky they are often referred to as storm clouds. Storm clouds can bring extreme weather hail, winds, lightning, hard rain, and tornadoes.

Write About   Write a paragraph telling about an experience you have had with extreme weather. Use a colon and semicolon correctly in your paragraph.

_____
_____
_____
_____
_____
_____
_____
_____

Review   Read each sentence. Write **C** on the line if the sentence is correct. If it is not, cross out any incorrect colons or semicolons. Insert colons and semicolons where they belong.

1. The train leaves at 6:18; we should be at the station by 6:05. _____

2. Please buy the party supplies; streamers, balloons, confetti, and the cake. _____

3. Most birds fly south for the winter: some do not. _____

4. Nina dropped her smartphone; now the screen is cracked. _____

5. The art teacher ordered new supplies: markers, paintbrushes, clay, and canvas. _____

6. Dad watches the news at 6;00: I usually watch with him. _____

Hyphens, Dashes, and Parentheses

Remember   A **hyphen (-)** separates the parts of some compound nouns and adjectives. It also sets off certain prefixes.

forty-two   brother-in-law   ex-president   low-key

Parentheses ( ) and **dashes (—)** set off information that interrupts the flow of a sentence. Dashes emphasize the extra information. Parentheses do not emphasize the information. Sometimes either mark works in a situation. You may make a choice based on style.

The puppy (the one with the red ball) is so cute.

A walk in the wood—look at the beautiful leaves!—is fun in the fall.

Think About   How many parentheses or dashes do you use for each interruption? Why do you think this is true?

_____

_____

Read and Apply   Read the sentences. Put parentheses, dashes, or hyphens where they belong.

The Galapagos batfish known as the red lipped batfish lives deep in the ocean near the Galapagos Islands. This odd looking fish some think it looks like a bat gets its name because it looks as if it uses red lipstick. A poor swimmer what type of fish doesn't swim well? the batfish uses its fins to walk along the bottom of the ocean. When it becomes an adult, the red lipped batfish's dorsal fin becomes a spine like projection. With this projection called an illicium , the batfish entices food its way. This small sized fish they are about 25 centimeters long eat crabs, mollusks, and other invertebrates.

Write About Write a paragraph about an unusual animal that you have seen.

_____

_____

_____

_____

_____

_____

_____

_____

Review Read each sentence. Write **C** on the line if the dashes, parentheses, and hyphens are used correctly. Write **N** if they are not used correctly.

1. Luke's sister-in-law (a teacher) explained the math problem. _____

2. My dad's custom-built car—it's bright orange!—goes very fast. _____

3. (After the break-in,) the neighborhood set up a nightly watch. _____

4. The annual fair—do you remember the date? is always a fun time. _____

5. One-half of the runners in the race will win a T-shirt. _____

6. Austin (an-ex-golfer) taught lessons at the club. _____

Lesson 1

UNIT 9: Choosing the Right Word

Homophones

Remember **Homophones** are words that sound alike but are spelled differently.
<u>Peace</u> was declared, and the war was over.
I lost a <u>piece</u> of the puzzle.

Think About Why is it important to use the correct spelling of a homophone?

_____

_____

Read and Apply Read the sentences. Cross out each incorrect homophone and write the correct word above it.

 The Greeks tell the tail of Daedalus and his son, Icarus. Daedalus was a great artist, and King Minos asked him too build a castle. As time past, King Minos became angry with Daedalus. It was knot fare, but the king locked Daedalus and Icarus in a tower. One day, a bird flu by the tower, and Daedalus had an idea. He maid a pear of wings for each of them. They would wear the wings and fly threw the air to safety.

 Daedalus warned Icarus to be careful. The wings were made of feathers and wax; if they flew too close to the son, the heat wood melt the wax. The two used there wings to soar into the sky. Icarus was sew excited. Higher and higher he rose. Daedalus cried out in vein as he saw his son's wings begin to melt. Too late, Icarus noticed as well. He fell into the see below and drowned.

Write About Write sentences using the pairs of homophones.

1. waist/waste

   _____
   _____

2. rain/reign

   _____
   _____

3. groan/grown

   _____
   _____

4. higher/hire

   _____
   _____

Review Read each sentence. Cross out the incorrect homophone in each sentence. Write the correct word on the line.

1. It is hard to know what to wear in this whether.   _____

2. The baker made bread and roles.   _____

3. Several kinds of breakfast seriel were on sale.   _____

4. A loan hare jumped across the plain.   _____

5. We herd some children singing.   _____

6. At night, the tied comes in.   _____

© The Continental Press, Inc.   DUPLICATING THIS MATERIAL IS ILLEGAL.

Avoiding Double Negatives

Remember Some words mean "no." These include *no, not, nothing, nobody, none,* and *never.* Other negative words include *hardly, barely,* and *scarcely.* Only one of these words should be used in a sentence. This is true even when the word *not* is part of a contraction.

Incorrect There aren't no cookies left in the jar.

Correct There are no cookies left in the jar.
There aren't any cookies left in the jar.

Think About Why is there usually more than one way to correct a sentence with a double negative?

_____

_____

Read and Apply Read the sentences. Correct any sentences with double negatives by crossing out words and replacing them as needed.

In the early 1900s, doctors didn't have no medicine to treat bacterial infections. Many people died because nobody had nothing with which to treat their illnesses. Scientists couldn't never find a treatment that killed the bacteria but didn't harm a human body. Then Alexander Fleming found a special mold. One day, in his laboratory, Fleming noticed that a certain mold had killed some bacteria. He couldn't hardly believe his eyes. He hadn't seen nothing like it before.

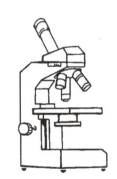

Useable treatment didn't scarcely come right away. It took years of research and development before a drug was created. Penicillin was the world's first antibiotic. Today, no one can't imagine life without it.

© The Continental Press, Inc. **DUPLICATING THIS MATERIAL IS ILLEGAL.**

Write About

Write a paragraph describing a time that you were ill and needed to visit a doctor or take medication. How do you imagine this was different than 100 years ago?

_____
_____
_____
_____
_____
_____
_____
_____
_____

Review

Listen to each sentence. Circle **CORRECT** if the sentence is correct. Circle **INCORRECT** if the sentence contains a double negative.

1. CORRECT   INCORRECT
2. CORRECT   INCORRECT
3. CORRECT   INCORRECT
4. CORRECT   INCORRECT
5. CORRECT   INCORRECT
6. CORRECT   INCORRECT

Misused Words

Remember *Don't* is the contraction for *do not*. It is used with a plural subject or the pronouns *I* and *you*. *Doesn't* is the contraction for *does not*. It is used with a singular subject.

Incorrect The girls <u>doesn't</u> know which way to go. Jamal <u>don't</u> know either.

Correct The girls <u>don't</u> know which way to go. Jamal <u>doesn't</u> know either.

The verb *go* refers to movement. It is not a conversation word.

Brianna ~~goes~~ says, "Please hold my jacket."

Think About When are these words most often misused?

Read and Apply Read the sentences. Find the five misused words. Cross out each misused word and write the correct word above it.

Bald eagle pairs usually mate for life, but if one dies or don't return to the nest, the other finds a new mate. Bald eagles don't change the location of their nest each year. After the female lays two to three eggs, the parents doesn't leave their eggs alone for long.

"I don't know very much about bald eagles," goes Sam.

Mandy says, "Eagles don't like human too close to their nests."

"What happens," Sam goes, "after the eggs hatch?"

"The mother don't hunt as much. She stays with the babies," says Mandy. "As the chicks grow, the parents don't feed them as much, so they learn to hunt. If the chick doesn't learn how to hunt, it will die."

© The Continental Press, Inc. DUPLICATING THIS MATERIAL IS ILLEGAL.

Write About Have a conversation with a friend about wild animals that you have observed. Discuss some of the things that these animals may or may not do. Record parts of the conversation using appropriate conversation words.

_____
_____
_____
_____
_____
_____
_____
_____

Review Read each sentence. Circle the correct word to complete each sentence.

1. My sister [don't   doesn't] know how to roller skate.

2. I [don't   doesn't] like salt on my vegetables.

3. When I told Tiffany about the movie, she [said   went], "Let's watch it!"

4. Our family [don't   doesn't] have a big backyard.

5. I [go   say], "I want to play baseball next year."

6. After eating a big meal, many people [don't   doesn't] have room for dessert.

Lesson 4: More Misused Words

Remember The verb *teach* means "to give instruction." The verb *learn* means "to receive instruction."

Dillon will <u>teach</u> me to play guitar. I hope I can <u>learn</u> quickly.

The verb *raise* means "to lift up" or "to increase or collect." It is a transitive verb. The verb *rise* means "to get up" or "to increase in amount." It is an intransitive verb.

Alexis <u>raises</u> her hand to ask a question. She <u>rises</u> from her seat to speak.

Think About How can you remember the difference between *raise* and *rise*?

_____

_____

Read and Apply Read the sentences. Find the five misused words. Cross out each misused word and write the correct word above it.

Jaime Escalante taught math in a tough Los Angeles high school. When he began, most of his students knew little math. He rose the standards; he made them want to learn. He encouraged them, telling the students that they could rise out of poverty. Soon, Escalante's students had taught as much as students in better schools. He learned one class a difficult form of math called calculus. In order for them to take an advanced calculus exam, Escalante raised the funds the students needed. Many of them passed the test. Each year, the number of students in his class raised. The students were eager to learn, and Escalante was excited to learn them. Many of his students went on to excel in college.

Write About   Write a paragraph about a teacher who made an impact on your life.

_____
_____
_____
_____
_____
_____
_____
_____
_____
_____

Review   Read each sentence. Circle the correct word to complete each sentence.

1. The price of gas continues to [raise   rise].

2. Cody [taught   learned] me to ride bike.

3. Abby wants to [teach   learn] to play the flute.

4. Will you help me [raise   rise] this banner over the stage?

5. The cat [raised   rose] from the windowsill and stretched.

6. Mr. Nelson [teaches   learns] his class about chemical elements.

Knowing the Difference

Remember The word *between* refers to two things. The word *among* refers to three or more things.

You can choose **between** chocolate or vanilla ice cream.

The ball is somewhere **among** those plants and bushes.

The noun *effect* means "the result of something." The verb *affect* means "to influence."

My late night had a negative **effect** on my test score.

Pollen really **affects** my allergies.

Think About How can you remember the difference between *effect* and *affect*?

_____

_____

Read and Apply Read the sentences. Find the five misused words. Cross out each misused word and write the correct word above it.

People have acknowledged the effect of music on mood for a long time. Now scientists are also recognizing that music affects people physically. When you choose among a soothing ballad and a loud rock song, your mood may be calmed or excited. Between researchers, studies look at how different songs effect people suffering from diseases. A patient with Parkinson's disease, which affects a person's muscle control, may move gracefully to a piece of music. Musicians with Tourette's syndrome, a disease that has the affect of muscle tics, effortlessly perform musical pieces. Their symptoms seem to momentarily disappear. People continue to study music's long-term affects on people's brains and bodies.

Write About Write a paragraph about a favorite piece of music and how you feel when you listen to it.

_____

_____

_____

_____

_____

_____

_____

_____

_____

_____

Review Read the sentences. Circle the correct word to complete each sentence.

1. My homework is somewhere [between   among] the papers in my backpack.

2. The predicted snowstorm [effected   affected] our plans for the weekend.

3. Working with a tutor had a positive [effect   affect] on Angel's test score.

4. Hang this picture [between   among] the doorway and the window.

5. The dog sat [between   among] me and the gate.

6. Changes in the weather [effect   affect] some people's health.

UNIT 10: Writing Letters
Writing a Thank-You Note

Remember   A friendly letter has five parts: the **heading,** a **greeting,** the **body,** a **closing,** and a **signature.** A **thank-you note** is a type of friendly letter. Write a thank-you note to show appreciation for something someone has given you or done for you.

Think About   What are two situations when it is appropriate to write a thank-you note?

_____

_____

Read and Apply   Read the thank-you note. Answer the questions below.

> 195A Cherry Avenue
> Macon, GA 31211
> August 2, 2017
>
> Dear Zoe,
>
>   Thank you for inviting me to come with your family to Tybee Island for a week. It was a lot of fun! My favorite part was when we rode bikes on the beach. I also loved swimming. Thanks again!
>
> Your friend,
> **Addy**

1. Who wrote the thank-you note? _____

2. When was the letter written? _____

3. Why are commas used in the heading? _____
   _____

4. Why was the thank-you note written? _____
   _____

© The Continental Press, Inc.   **DUPLICATING THIS MATERIAL IS ILLEGAL.**

Write About Write a thank-you note to someone. Use your address and today's date in the heading. Be sure to include all five parts of a friendly letter. Capitalize and punctuate correctly.

_____
_____
_____
_____
_____
_____
_____
_____
_____
_____
_____
_____
_____
_____
_____
_____
_____
_____

Review Read the body of each thank-you note. Cross out the information that should not be included.

1. Thank you for coming to my orchestra concert at school. We were all very excited to play. I think that I should have had the violin solo. I really enjoy learning to play violin. It was nice to have people support me at my concert. Thanks again!

2. Thank you for sending me a birthday present. It was fun to get a surprise gift in the mail. I am looking forward to spending the gift card to buy some clothes for school. If the gift card was for more money, I could buy the jacket I really want. It was kind of you to send me a gift. Thanks so much.

Writing an Invitation

Remember An **invitation** is a type of friendly letter. It asks someone to come to an event. It should include the event's important information: type of event, time, place, and RSVP information. To RSVP to an invitation means the person being invited tells the host or hostess if he or she is able to come.

Think About Why does a host or hostess ask people to RSVP?

_____
_____

Read and Apply Read the invitation. Answer the questions below.

> 89 Huntsville Drive
> Florence, AL 35630
> October 18, 2017
>
> Dear Nate,
>
> You're invited to a surprise birthday party for Logan Mitchell! It is on Sunday, November 5, 2017, at 2:30 pm. Please come on time. Logan will come at 3:00. Call me at 256-204-4321 by October 27 to let me know if you can come. Hope you will be there!
>
> Your friend,
> **Jerome**

1. What is the event? _____

2. What information is missing? _____

3. How should Nate RSVP? _____

4. What is the date for the event? _____

© The Continental Press, Inc.   **DUPLICATING THIS MATERIAL IS ILLEGAL.**

Write About Write an invitation to someone. Write your address and today's date in the heading. Include all the five parts of a friendly letter. Be sure the invitation includes all the important information for the event. Capitalize and punctuate correctly.

_____
_____
_____
_____
_____
_____
_____
_____
_____

Review Read this invitation. Cross out any unnecessary information. Add commas where they belong. If there is important information that is missing, write what it is on the line below.

> 903 Riverside Drive
> Apartment 102
> Pittsburgh PA 15206
> February 1 2018
>
> Dear Leilani
>
>   You are invited to a Valentine's Day party on February 16 2018. Come to my home at 6:30 pm and bring a red snack to share with everyone. Do you understand what we are learning in science class? I hope you can come!
>
>   Your friend
>   **Sierra**

_____

Writing a Business Letter

Remember A **business letter** has a different form than a friendly letter. Write the **inside address** between the heading and the greeting. Use a **colon (:)** after the greeting. Print the writer's name under the written signature.

> heading: 408 Silverton Way
> Springfield, PA 19064
> March 12, 2018
>
> Beans and More Coffee Company
> 836 Main Street, Suite B
> Springfield, PA 19064   } inside address
>
> Dear Sir or Madam: } greeting
>
> I visited your coffee shop on March 8, 2018. I did not have a good experience. I did not receive the type of drink I ordered. The one I did get was cold. The people who were working there were rude. I will not be coming back to your coffee shop.   } body
>
> Sincerely, } closing
> *Carla Hedrick*
> Carla Hedrick   } signature

Think About What is the tone of a business letter?

_____

Read and Apply Read the letter in the example above again. Answer these questions.

1. Who wrote the letter? _____

2. What company is receiving the letter? _____

3. Why is there no person named in the greeting? _____
   _____

4. What is the purpose of the letter? _____

5. How is the closing different from the closing in a friendly letter? _____
   _____

© The Continental Press, Inc.   **DUPLICATING THIS MATERIAL IS ILLEGAL.**

Write About Write a business letter below. Use your address and today's date in the heading. Write the letter to Star Electronics, P.O. Box 6014, New York, New York 10007. Express displeasure with a tablet computer you recently purchased from them.

___

Review Answer these questions about business letters.

1. What part contains the address of the person or company to whom the letter is being sent?

2. How is the tone of a business letter different from the tone of a friendly letter?

3. What details should you include when telling about a bad experience or a bad product?

Addressing an Envelope

Remember   Write the **return address** in the upper left corner of an envelope. Write the **mailing address** in the middle. Put a stamp in the upper right corner.

Return Address:
Ella Kato
P.O. Box 2596
Wausau, WI 54401

Stamp →

Mailing Address:
Mr. William Bechtel, Editor
The Daily News
5469 North King Street, Suite 209
Wausau, WI 54401

Think About   Why might an address have four lines instead of three?

_____

_____

_____

Read and Apply   Read the envelope below. Add the correct punctuation where needed. List the missing information on the line below.

Prof J Marks
South University
165 Harper Blvd
Phoenix AZ 85065

Ms S L Shirk
8634 19th St NW
Washington DC

Write About Address the envelope below correctly. Use your name, school's name, and school's address for the return address. Write this name and address correctly for the mailing address: mr d cramer art supplies inc 81 lompa square carson city nv 89701. Draw a stamp in the correct place.

Review Answer these questions about addressing an envelope.

1. What information is on the last line of an address? _____

2. Which address is written in the middle of the envelope? _____

3. What punctuation marks are used in an address and where are they placed?
_____
_____

Writing an Email

Remember Many people communicate with email for personal and business use. Maintain proper grammar when communicating electronically. The **subject line** of an email should clearly state the email's purpose.

```
To: artdesigns@artstore.com
From: mlopez23@email.com
Subject: Order #580367
```

New   Send   Reply   Attach

To Whom It May Concern:

I placed order #580367 on January 9, 2017. I received a confirmation email, but I still have not received the order. It was supposed to take 2–3 weeks to arrive, and it has now been 5 weeks. Please check the status of my order. Thank you for your help.

Miguel Lopez
Account #T69084

Think About What important information that is included in a business or friendly letter is automatically attached to an email?

_____
_____

Read and Apply Read the email above again. Answer the questions below.

1. From what email address is the email being sent? _____

2. What is the subject line of the email? _____

3. To what email address is the email being sent? _____

4. What is the purpose of the email? _____
_____

Write About Write an email to the owner of Sweet Treats Bakery to ask if she will make a donation to your soccer team's bake sale fundraiser. Include an appropriate subject line. Create an email address using your name.

To: cassie@sweettreats.biz
From:
Subject:

New   Send   Reply   Attach

Review Read this text from an email. Edit the text for proper grammar, including capitalization, punctuation, word usage, and missing words.

mrs fisher

i are interested in the part-time position in your flower shop I really like to work with flowers and learn more about growing and arranging it this would be my first job. I am hard worker and a fast learn. I like to help people and I enjoy learn new things. I would appreciate the chance to have an interview

thank you

julia martin

Writing a Review

Remember   Many websites provide opportunities to write reviews for goods or services that you have received. A **review** is a way for you to tell others your opinion of a product or a company. A helpful review should be specific about what was good and bad. It should use correct grammar. It should not be full of anger or name-calling. Avoid exaggerations.

Think About   Why is it important to be specific in an online review?

_____

_____

Read and Apply   Read the review. Cross out the information that is not important. Underline the information that should be more specific. Circle the information that is exaggerated.

© The Continental Press, Inc.   **DUPLICATING THIS MATERIAL IS ILLEGAL.**

Write About

Write a review about a new movie theater. Tell about your experience there. Be specific about what you liked or disliked.

_____
_____
_____
_____
_____
_____
_____
_____
_____
_____
_____
_____

Review

Read the review below. Then rewrite the review using correct grammar and spelling. Remove inappropriate content and add details to explain your opinion.

I brought this shirt in green. The color was very bright and prety. But the shirt wasnt no good. It wasnt comfortable. I didnt like it it was the worst shirt in the world!!!!

_____
_____
_____
_____
_____

Grammar Handbook

Abbreviation	a short way to write a word, usually ending in a period. Abbreviations for proper nouns begin with a capital letter.
	Examples: Jan. Thurs. Rd.
Abstract Noun	a noun that you cannot see, smell, taste, touch, or hear
	Examples: friendship loyalty pride
Action Verb	a word that tells about doing something
	Examples: grin imagines went
Adjective	a word that describes a noun by telling how many, what color, what size, or what kind
	Examples: three bikes tiny cat
Adjective Clause	a dependent clause that acts as an adjective in a sentence, modifying a noun or pronoun
Adverb	a word that describes a verb, adjective, or another adverb by telling how, when, or where something happened
	Examples: run slowly play today very happy
Adverb Clause	a dependent clause that acts as an adverb in a sentence
Antecedent	the noun that a pronoun takes the place of
Apostrophe	a punctuation mark that takes the place of letters left out of a contraction or makes a possessive form
Appositive	a word or group of words that explains or identifies a noun or pronoun before or after it. It is set off from the sentence with commas.
Articles	the special adjectives *a*, *an*, and *the*
Body	the main part of a letter
Business Letter	a letter written to someone the sender does not know for a reason that is not personal

Clause	a group of words that has a subject and a predicate
Closing	the part of a letter that says good-bye
Collective Noun	a noun that names a group of people or things

> *Examples:* team   army   family

Colon	a punctuation mark used to introduce a list or after the greeting in a business letter
Comma	a punctuation mark that separates things or ideas
Comparative	form of an adjective or adverb that compares two
Complete Predicate	the simple predicate and all the words that tell about it
Complete Subject	the simple subject and all the words that tell about it
Complex Sentence	a sentence with two parts: a dependent clause and an independent clause
Compound Predicate	two predicates joined together in one sentence with the word *and*
Compound Sentence	two sentences joined together with the word *and, but, or,* or *so*
Compound Subject	two subjects joined together in one sentence with the word *and*
Compound-Complex Sentence	a sentence that contains two or more independent clauses and at least one dependent clause
Concrete Noun	a noun that you can see, hear, taste, touch, or smell
Conjunction	a connecting word

> *Examples:* and   or   but

Contraction	two words combined into one by using an apostrophe to take the place of the letters left out

> *Examples:* he'll   wouldn't   can't

Coordinate Adjectives	adjectives that appear as a group to modify the same noun

> *Examples:* the big, blue plastic ball

Coordinating Conjunction	conjunctions that join ideas of equal importance

Dangling Modifier	a modifier that does not clearly belong to any word in the sentence
Dash	a punctuation mark used to show a break in the flow of a sentence
Declarative Sentence	a sentence that tells something
Demonstrative Adjective	an adjective that points out a noun

> *Examples:*   this   that   these   those

Dependent Clause	part of a sentence that has a subject and a predicate but does not make sense by itself
Direct Object	a noun or pronoun that receives the action of an action verb
Direct Quotation	the exact words that someone said
Exclamation Point	the punctuation mark used at the end of an exclamatory sentence
Exclamatory Sentence	a sentence that shows strong feeling
Fragment	a group of words that does not tell a complete thought
Future Tense	a verb tense that tells about action that will happen later
Greeting	the part near the beginning of a letter that names the person receiving it
Heading	the part at the beginning of a letter that gives the writer's address and the date the letter was written
Helping Verb	a verb that helps a main verb tell about an action

> *Examples:*   has arrived   is sleeping

Homophones	words that sound alike, but are spelled differently and have different meanings
Hyphen	a punctuation mark used to join the parts of some compound nouns and compound adjectives, and to join some prefixes with their root words

> *Examples:*   a friendly-looking person   pre-exist

Imperative Sentence	a sentence that tells or commands someone to do something
Indefinite Pronoun	a pronoun that does not refer to a specific noun

> *Examples:* anyone   somebody   many

Independent Clause	part of a sentence with a subject and a predicate that makes sense by itself
Indirect Object	a noun or pronoun that receives the direct object
Indirect Quotation	the idea but not the exact words that a person spoke
Initial	the first letter of a name
Inside Address	the name and address of the person receiving a business letter
Intensifier	an adverb that adds emphasis or strong meaning
Intensive Pronoun	a *self*-pronoun that is used for emphasis, it follows the noun or pronoun it refers to
Interjection	a word that shows strong or sudden feeling
Interrogative Pronoun	a pronoun that is used to ask a question

> *Examples:* who   whom   which

Interrogative Sentence	a sentence that asks a question
Intransitive Verb	a verb that does not have a direct object
Invitation	a type of friendly letter asking a person to come to an event
Linking Verb	a verb that tells about being something, does not show action

> *Examples:* is   were   are

Mailing Address	the address a letter is being sent to
Main Verb	the most important verb in a sentence
Misplaced Modifier	a modifier that is incorrectly located in a sentence and causes confusion
Modifier	a word or group of words that adds details to the sentence
Noun	a person, place, animal, or thing
Noun Clause	a dependent clause that acts as a noun in a sentence

Object of a Preposition	the noun or pronoun that follows a preposition
Object Pronoun	form of a pronoun that the action is happening to
Parentheses	punctuation marks that surround extra information in a sentence
Past Participle	a special past-tense verb form used with the helping verbs *has, have,* and *had*
Past Tense	a verb tense that tells about action that already happened
Perfect Tense	a verb tense that uses helping verbs and the past participle of the main verb to describe action
Period	the punctuation mark used at the end of a declarative or imperative sentence and most abbreviations
Plural Noun	a noun that names more than one person, place, animal, or thing
	Examples: trees benches children
Possessive Noun	a noun that names who or what something belongs to
	Examples: Jody's desk dogs' bones
Possessive Pronoun	a pronoun that names who or what something belongs to
	Examples: my shoes its tail
Predicate	the part of a sentence that tells what the subject does or is
Predicate Adjective	an adjective following a linking verb in the predicate of a sentence that describes the subject
Predicate Noun	a noun following a linking verb in the predicate of a sentence that refers back to the simple subject
Preposition	a word that relates the noun or pronoun that follows it to another word in the sentence
	Examples: after by from with
Prepositional Phrase	a preposition, the noun or pronoun that follows it, and all the words that come between them
Present Participle	a special verb form made by adding *ing* to the verb that is used with a helping verb
Present Tense	a verb tense that describes action taking place now

Progressive Tense	a verb tense that uses a helping verb and the present participle of the main verb to show continuing action
Pronoun	a word that can take the place of a noun

> *Examples:* she   he   it

Proper Adjective	an adjective based on a proper noun

> *Examples:* Canadian border   Florida sunset

Proper Noun	a word that names a special person, place, animal, or thing

> *Examples:* Ellie   Nevada   Fido   Mayflower

Question Mark	the punctuation mark used at the end of an interrogative sentence
Quotation Marks	punctuation marks used before and after someone's exact words in a written conversation
Reflexive Pronoun	a *self*-pronoun that refers back to the subject of the sentence

> *Examples:* himself   themselves

Relative Pronoun	a pronoun that starts a description of a noun

> *Examples:* who   which   whose

Return Address	the address from which a letter is being sent
Review	a piece of writing, often posted on the Internet, that describes what is good or bad about a product or service
Run-On Sentence	a group of words that tells more than one complete thought without appropriate punctuation
Semicolon	a punctuation mark used to join two independent clauses
Sentence	a group of words that tells a complete thought and makes sense
Signature	the writer's name at the end of a letter
Simple Predicate	the verb or verb phrase that tells what the subject does or is
Simple Subject	the noun or pronoun that the sentence tells about

Single Quotation Marks	a type of punctuation mark that surrounds a direct quotation inside another direct quotation
Singular Noun	a noun that names one person, place, animal, or thing

    Examples: tree   bench   child

Subject	the part of a sentence that tells who or what the sentence is about
Subject Line	the part of an email that tells what it is about
Subject Pronoun	form of a pronoun that appears in the subject part of a sentence
Subordinate Conjunction	a conjunction that connects an independent and dependent clause

    Examples: before   even if   than

Superlative	form of an adjective or adverb that compares three or more
Thank-You Note	a type of friendly letter expressing thanks
Title	part of a person's name or the name of a book or story

    Examples: Miss Brown   Dr. Sanchez
                        Alice in Wonderland   "Cinderella"

Transitive Verb	a verb that has a direct object
Uncountable Nouns	nouns that cannot be counted with numbers, always expressed as singular

    Examples: soup   news   water

Verb Phrase	the main verb and any helping verbs

    Examples: were laughing   are running

USING CAPITAL LETTERS

- Begin every sentence with a capital letter.
- Begin each part of a person's name with a capital letter. Include titles that are used as part of the name and initials.
- Begin words that name days, months, holidays, and places with a capital letter. Do not capitalize the names of seasons. Do not capitalize articles, the conjunction *and,* or prepositions such as *of* and *for* in proper nouns.

USING PUNCTUATION MARKS

End Marks

- End a statement with a period.
- End a question with a question mark.
- End an exclamation with an exclamation point.

Commas

- Use a comma before the joining word in a compound sentence.
- Use commas between words or phrases in a series.
- Use a comma between the day and year in a date.
- Use a comma between a city and state.
- Use a comma to separate an appositive from the rest of the sentence.
- Use a comma after a dependent clause when it comes at the beginning of a sentence.

Apostrophes

- Use an apostrophe to show who owns or has something. If the owner is singular, add an apostrophe and *s*. If the owner is plural and ends in *s,* add just an apostrophe.
- Use an apostrophe to show where letters are missing in a contraction.

Quotation Marks

- Use quotation marks before and after a person's exact words.
- Use single quotation marks around a direct quotation in another direct quotation.
- When phrases such as *he said* come after a quotation, end the quotation with a comma unless it is a question or an exclamation. Put the comma, question mark, or exclamation point inside the quotation marks.

Colons
- Use a colon to introduce a list in a sentence.
- Use a colon after the greeting of a business letter.

Semicolons
- Use a semicolon to separate independent clauses in a compound sentence. The semicolon takes the place of a conjunction.

Dashes
- Use a dash to show an interruption in the flow of a sentence. Dashes are used in pairs. Put one dash at the beginning of the interruption and one dash at the end. A dash emphasizes the interruption.

Parentheses
- Use parentheses around information that disrupts the flow of a sentence. Parentheses are used in pairs; they do not call extra attention to the interruption.

Hyphens
- Use a hyphen to form some compound nouns or adjectives. Use it to join some prefixes with their root words.

Showing Titles
- Capitalize the first word, last word, and every important word in a title.
- Underline or use italics for book, newspaper, magazine, play, and movie titles.
- Use quotation marks for shorter works, such as poems, stories, TV shows, songs, and articles.

USING CORRECT GRAMMAR

Subject-Verb Agreement
- When you use an action verb in the present tense, add *s* or *es* to the verb if the subject is a singular noun. Do not add *s* or *es* to the verb if the subject is plural.
- If the subject is a pronoun, add *s* or *es* to the verb only if the pronoun is *he*, *she*, or *it*.

© The Continental Press, Inc.   **DUPLICATING THIS MATERIAL IS ILLEGAL.**

Subject-Verb Agreement with Forms of *Be*

- If the subject is a singular noun, use *is* for the present tense and *was* for the past tense.
- If the subject is a plural noun or compound subject, use *are* for the present tense and *were* for the past tense.
- Use the correct form of *be* with a singular or plural pronoun subject.

Present Tense		Past Tense	
Singular	**Plural**	**Singular**	**Plural**
I am you are he, she, *or* it is	we are you are they are	I was you were he, she, *or* it was	we were you were they were

Irregular Verbs

- The verbs below and many others are called irregular because their past-tense forms do not end in *ed*. Use the correct past-tense forms and past participles of irregular verbs.

Present	Past	Past Participle
is	was	(has) been
begin	began	(has) begun
bring	brought	(has) brought
choose	chose	(has) chosen
come	came	(has) come
fly	flew	(has) flown
go	went	(has) gone
have	had	(has) had
know	knew	(has) known
make	made	(has) made
run	ran	(has) run
say	said	(has) said
speak	spoke	(has) spoken
take	took	(has) taken
wear	wore	(has) worn
write	wrote	(has) written

Subject and Object Pronouns

- Pronouns have different subject and object forms.
- Use subject pronouns as the subject of a sentence.
- Use object pronouns after an action verb or after a preposition such as *of, to, for,* or *about*. The pronouns *you* and *it* have only one form.

Subject		Object	
Singular	Plural	Singular	Plural
I he she	we they	me him her	us them

Naming Yourself Last

- When you speak of yourself and another person, name yourself last.

Possessive Pronouns

- Use these possessive pronouns before a noun to show ownership.

Singular	Plural
my your his, her, its	our your their

- Use these possessive pronouns when a noun does not follow.

Singular	Plural
mine yours his, hers, its	ours yours theirs

Indefinite Pronouns

- Indefinite pronouns do not refer to a specific noun. The chart shows some examples.

Singular		Plural
anybody anything each everyone	everything nobody somebody something	all both few many some several

© The Continental Press, Inc.   **DUPLICATING THIS MATERIAL IS ILLEGAL.**

Reflexive and Intensive Pronouns

- Reflexive pronouns refer back to the sentence's subject. Intensive pronouns are used for emphasis.

Singular	Plural
myself	ourselves
yourself	yourselves
himself, herself, itself	themselves

Tricky Words

- Some words are often confused. Remember to use these words correctly.

a/an	Use *a* before a consonant sound. Use *an* before a vowel sound. Wrong: **a** orange Correct: **an** orange
affect/effect	Use *affect* as a verb: His bad grades **affected** his place on the football team. Use *effect* as a noun: The **effects** of the storm are still seen today.

can/may	Use *can* to ask if or tell that you are able to do something. Use *may* to ask if or tell that something is possible or allowed.
	  Wrong: **Can** I borrow your pen?
	  Correct: **May** I borrow your pen?

good/well	Use *good* only as an adjective. Use *well* as an adverb unless you are describing someone's state of health.
	  Wrong: He pitches **good**.
	  Correct: He pitches **well**. He is a **good** pitcher.
	  Wrong: I have a cold and don't feel **good**.
	  Correct: I have a cold and don't feel **well**.

have/of	Use *have* or *'ve* after words such as *could, should,* and *would*. Do not use *of*.
	  Wrong: I could **of** gone.
	  Correct: I could **have** gone. I could**'ve** gone.

hear/here	*Hear* means "to be aware of sound": I **hear** music. *Here* means "in this place": Put your bags **here**.
its/it's	*Its* means "belonging to it": The dog wagged **its** tail. *It's* means "it is": **It's** raining.
let/leave	*Let* means "to allow": My parents **let** me stay up late. *Leave* means "to go away" or "to cause to remain": We must **leave** at 6:00. **Leave** your jacket at home.
raise/rise	*Raise* means "to lift up": **Raise** the banner over the door. *Rise* means "to get up": The dog **rises** from its bed.

teach/learn	*Teach* means "to give instruction": Please **teach** me to play the game. *Learn* means "to receive instruction": I want to **learn** the game.
than/then	*Than* is a word for comparing: Today is hotter **than** yesterday. *Then* means "at that time" or "next": Raise one arm and **then** the other.
their/there/they're	*Their* means "belonging to them": They ate **their** dinner. *There* means "in that place": **There** you are! Sit over **there**. *They're* means "they are": **They're** the fastest runners.
those/them	*Those* is an adjective that points out a noun: Bring **those** books with you. *Them* is an object pronoun: I went to the game with **them**.

to/too/two	*To* means "toward" or "for the purpose of":
	   Go **to** the park **to** play.
	To can also be part of a verb form: She likes **to** skate.
	Too means "more than enough" or "also":
	   I ate **too** much. You did, **too.**
	Two means "the sum of 1 + 1": The cat had **two** kittens.

who/whom	*Who* is a pronoun used as a subject of a sentence or a clause:
	   Who found the key?
	   I know **who** found the key.
	Whom is a pronoun used as an object in a sentence or a clause:
	   Whom did you ask?
	   Morgan is the one **whom** I asked.

who's/whose	*Who's* means "who is": **Who's** coming to the party? *Whose* is the possessive form of *who*: I don't know **whose** hat this is.
your/you're	*Your* means "belonging to you": Put on **your** jacket. *You're* means "you are": **You're** late for the bus.

NOTES